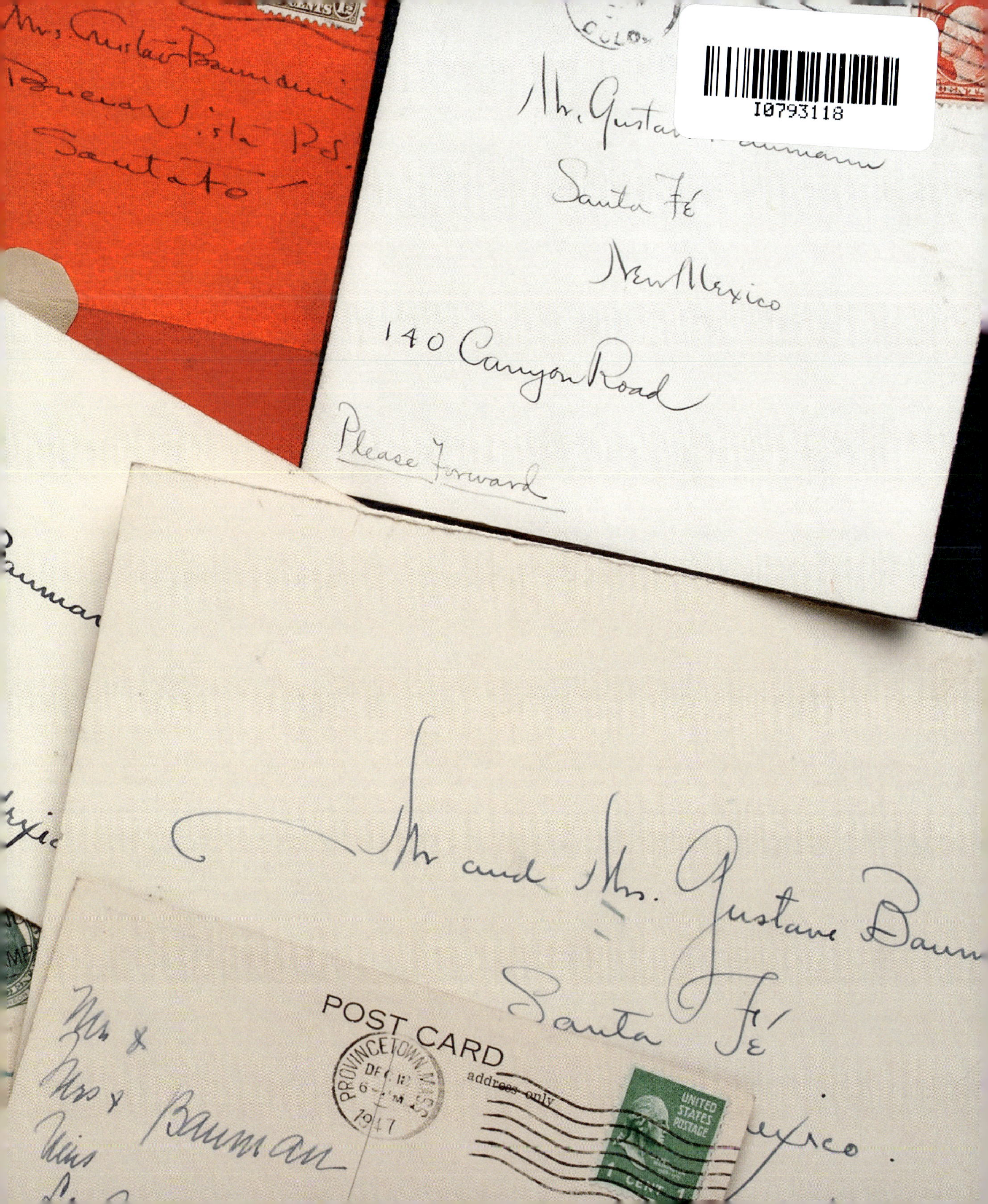

Santa Fé
New Mexico
140 Canyon Road
Please Forward
Mr and Mrs. Gustave Baum
Santa Fé
POST CARD
PROVINCETOWN MASS
1947
address only
UNITED STATES POSTAGE
Bauman

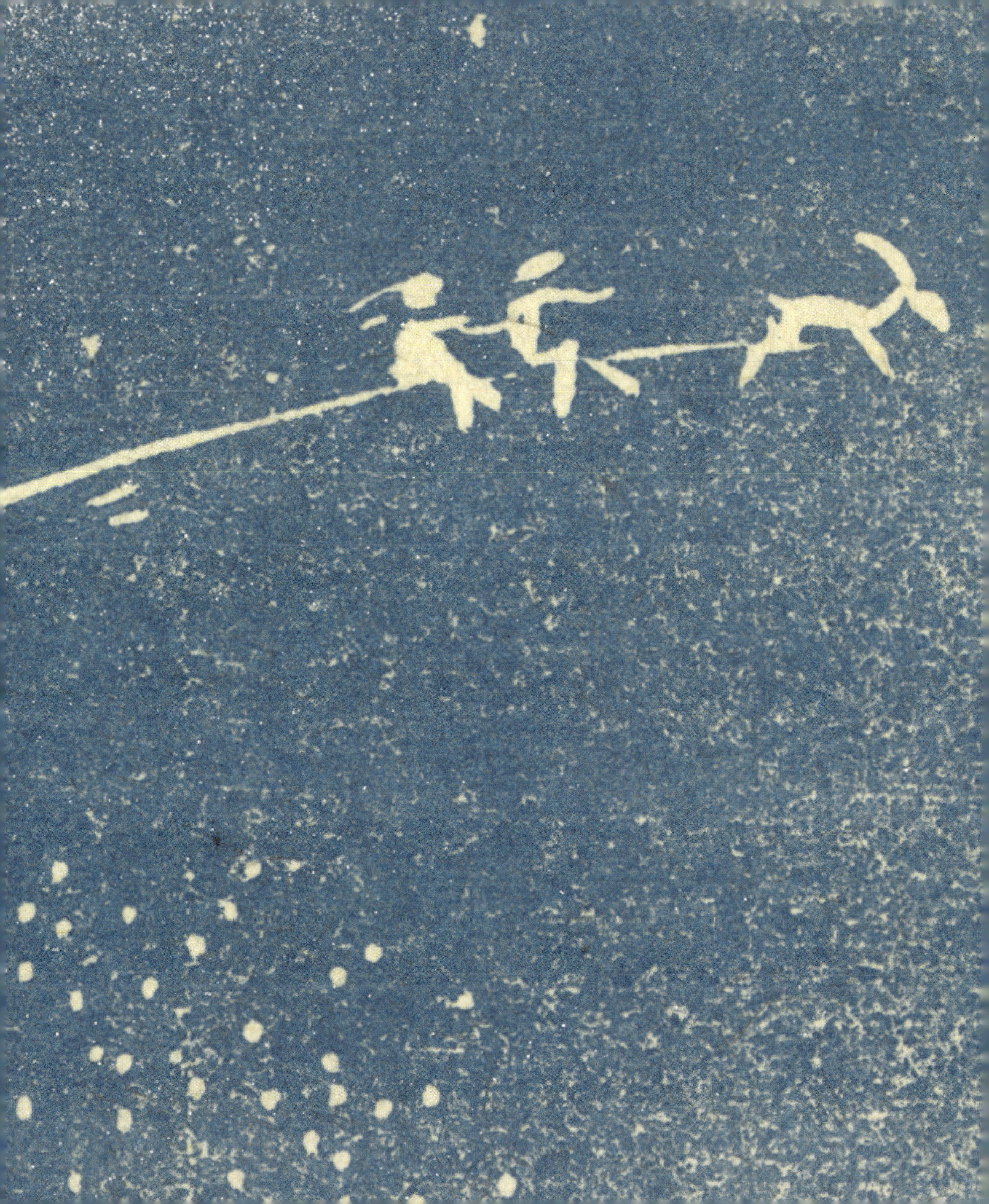

Gustave Baumann and Friends

ARTIST CARDS
FROM HOLIDAYS PAST

By Jean Moss
and Thomas Leech

Museum of New Mexico Press

Santa Fe

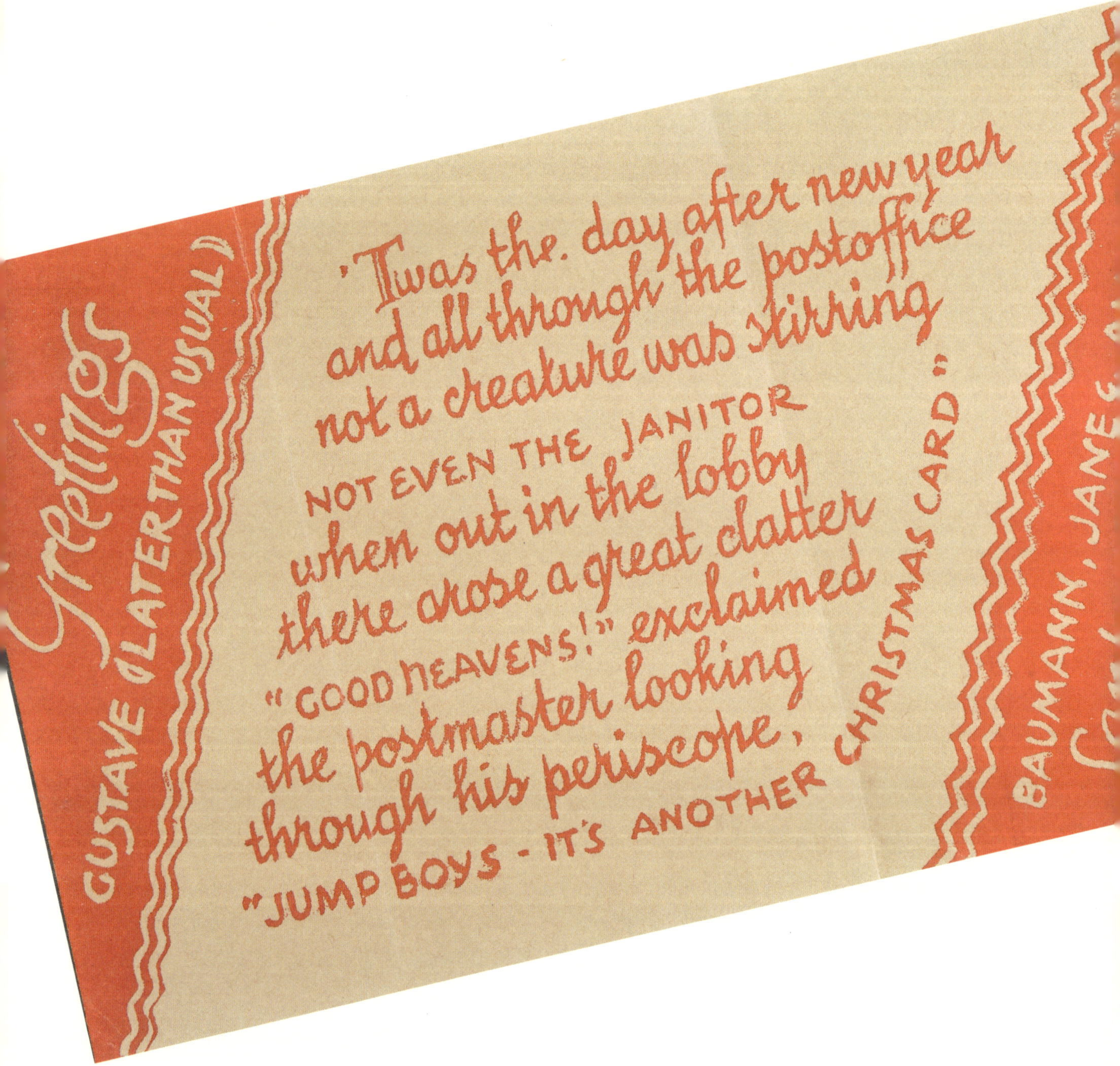
Greetings

GUSTAVE (LATER THAN USUAL)

'Twas the day after new year
and all through the postoffice
not a creature was stirring
NOT EVEN THE JANITOR
when out in the lobby
there arose a great clatter
"GOOD HEAVENS!" exclaimed
the postmaster looking
through his periscope,
"JUMP BOYS - IT'S ANOTHER CHRISTMAS CARD"

BAUMANN, JANE

Contents

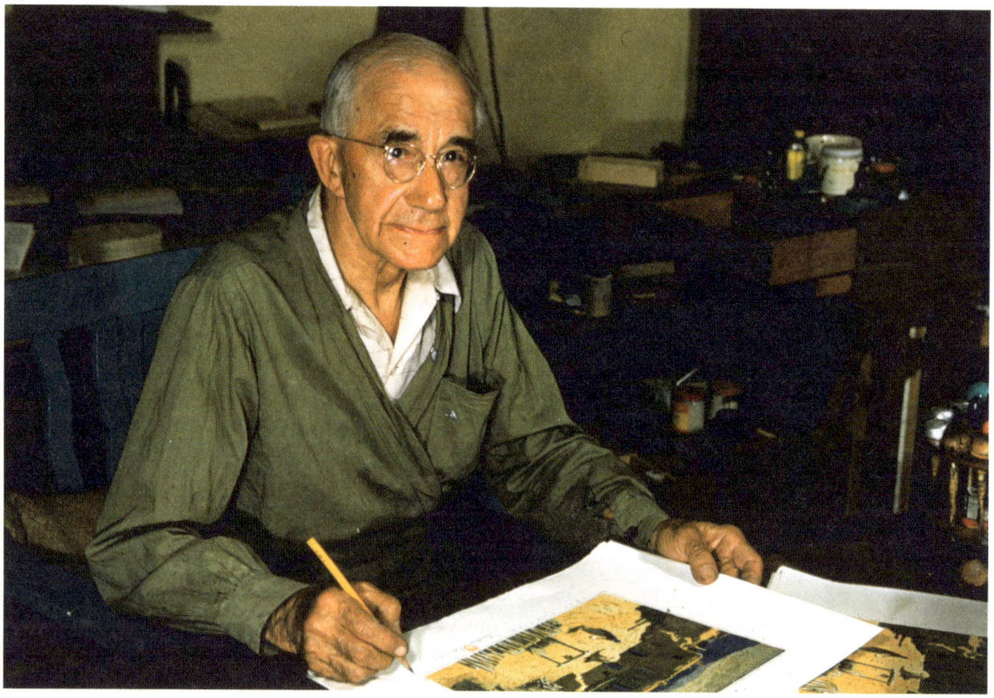

Gustave Baumann photographed in his studio, ca. 1960.

Greetings
and All That Sort of Thing

Once upon a time I thought I would never care to see another Christmas card. But happily, that was long ago. For those who still harbor notions that Christmas cards are made somewhere near the North Pole by artisan elves under the benevolent eye of a Gutenberg-like Santa, here is a different picture.

I can recall summer nights as a pressroom apprentice, the heat well over a hundred degrees; noise at ear-piercing decibels; the swoon-inducing smell of unknown and unpronounceable solvents; printing presses as large as buses gulping down five-pound cans of colored ink in minutes; cards with multiple Santa and Mrs. Clauses and reindeer and baby Jesuses and millions of identical snowflakes laid out thirty-two to a sheet, five thousand sheets an hour in a ten-hour shift; pallets and pallets of paper, measured by the ton, shooting through the press and disappearing into the night. Then at three in the morning the shift ended and a dozen exhausted guys staggered out under the stars, glad to be free from the glare of the more-Scrooge-than-Santa foreman to swallow fresh air and cold beer to erase the taste of the chemicals and all that sweet, sweet holiday cheer. Yes, Virginia, that is where Christmas cards come from.

For most of the history of Christmas cards, going all the way back to the very first card printed in Dickens-era England, the vast majority were produced in commercial printing establishments. And while the technologies of their manufacture have advanced (and continue to do so), I can't help but feel that the atmosphere of the pressrooms in which they were made varied little from that described above. So it is with great pleasure and much relief that the story we present here is considerably more pleasant. You might even call it enchanting.

Just as there are collections of matchbooks, bottle caps, and rubber bands, there are collections of Christmas cards. No doubt some of those card collections are historically significant, but the collection recently bequeathed to the New Mexico History Museum by the Ann Baumann Trust is notable enough to merit a book and an exhibition. What makes this collection so unusual is that these cards, for the most part, were created by artists, for artists, and likely in the quiet solitude of homes, studios, or even around kitchen tables.

The collection contains more than four hundred pieces from artists spread far and wide, and selecting from that trove was no easy task. A few of those faraway masters are presented, but our focus is on thirty-four New Mexican artists, working between 1918 and 1970. This is only a fraction of the artists who were active in the state during this period. Of the thirty-four, it seems that none made cards every year, save for one—Gustave Baumann—and he is the central character in this Christmas story. And what a character he was!

Artist, printer, painter, puppeteer, and . . . a list of his skills could fill a page. But wait—did I call Baumann a printer?! Calling Maestro Baumann a printer is like calling Tiffany a jeweler or Stravinsky a musician. Although you will not find "Baumann's Greatest Hits" in this collection of holiday cards, you will see him at his most playful. He may be carving with one hand behind his back, but he is also winking at us at the same time. Trying to divine his character from photographs, we're left wondering if he was a wise old owl or just a wise guy.

True to the nature of a puppeteer or a stage designer (yes, he did that, too), Baumann was most comfortable behind the scenes and out of the limelight. It would be a mistake to think that there was ever a "Baumann circle," yet he was an important contributor to a number of intersecting artistic and civic circles. Like other of his artist friends, Baumann trained in the commercial art and printing houses of Chicago and came to New Mexico as a "refugee" from industrial printing. (One friend turned his back on commercial art when he was told to make a drawing of a ham look more "graceful.") Some found ways of converting their technical skills directly to artistic expression, and when the holidays came they bypassed hired designers, lithographers, salespeople, and catalogs. Theirs was a direct line from the artist to the postman to the happy recipient, who was often another artist, which is not to say that they were not also sent to family and friends in all walks of life.

There seems not to have been a great need for the artists to show off their talents to one another. Probably all of the senders and receivers were well acquainted, and all knew the "serious" work that each pursued. So why be serious at all? While there are some truly virtuoso performances in the collection, whimsy and secular salutations were as much a part of the messages as seasonal greetings. One of my favorite pieces is the Baumann card for the 1935 New Year, printed in hot pink and black. The outside reads, "Greetings and all that sort of thing." On the inside is a nonsensical poem emblazoned across an image of Baumann's Billy the Kid birdbath. Not very Christmassy, and certainly not the kind of thing that would get by an art director at Hallmark!

Artist-made cards were another way of having fun, and Baumann worked at having fun. Evidence of his humor was never far from view. Our chronology begins with Gus's 1919 Christmas card, which carries on the back the Koshare pressmark he created and used as a personal logo well into his long life. The Koshare—what anthropologist Adolph Bandelier called the Delight Makers and called by others "sacred clowns"— were central to his character, just as they were central to the traditions of the Pueblo cultures that Baumann tried to fathom. To this day a gilded iron ornament gleams atop Baumann's Santa Fe home—a winking clown face made from the scrambled letters

K-O-S-H-A-R-E. For Gus, perhaps "delight" was a play on words (and I would not put the pun past him). Some artists came to New Mexico for the light; Baumann came for "de-light." And it is that delight we wish to share with you here.

Thomas Leech
Curator of the Press at the Palace of the Governors

A Word About
Dates and Techniques

It was not always easy to determine the dates of these cards. Some cards were sent prior to Christmas of a given year, with the year printed as part of the image, so dating was obvious. But some cards were postdated and sent after Christmas. Others were intended as New Year greetings but may have been created in the previous year. Other cards were created well into the new year, were dated in pencil by the artist, or were identified with a postmark. And finally, some cards simply were undated. We hope that with more time and research other examples will turn up definitive information.

Even with lifetimes spent looking at prints, and with magnifying glasses in hand, at times the authors still had to resort to their "best guesses." In most cases the description of the technique used to make a card is self-evident. Terms like woodcut, linoleum cut, lithograph, and etching are common enough not to require explanations here. But many of the cards combine techniques or use less well-known processes. The difference between a woodcut and a two-color woodcut is that in the latter two separate blocks are used to create the image. A hand-colored woodcut uses one block but the artist embellishes the print with another medium. A photo-engraving allows a drawing to be transferred to a metal printing plate but is then printed in the same manner as a wood or linoleum cut. The differences between a woodcut and a wood engraving lie in the kinds of tools used to create the image, and in which part of the grain is worked. A serigraph is another name for a silk screen print. We have tried to be consistent, but artists have a way of defying simple definitions.

Acknowledgments

This book could not have been completed without the enthusiastic support and participation of Gala Chamberlain and Daniel Lienau of the Annex Galleries in Santa Rosa, California, and to the following individuals and organizations: Bunny Huffman of The Women's International Study Center; Robert Bell, M.D. and the Bell Family Collection; Jerry West; Nancy Wirth; Kevin Ryan; Laura Holt of the School for Advanced Research; David Witt at the Academy for the Love of Learning; Tomas Jaehn and Patricia Hewitt of the Fray Angélico Chávez History Library; Daniel Kosharek and Hannah Abelbeck in the Palace of the Governors Photo Archives; Michelle Roberts, Rebecca Potance, and Erica Prater at the New Mexico Museum of Art; James Bourland at the Palace Press; and the staff of the Museum of New Mexico Press. Additional thanks to David Margolis, Kathleen Koltes, and David and Carol Farmer.

The Press at the Palace of the Governors has replicated a corner of Baumann's studio using his printing press, furniture, pigments for inks, unused papers, and hand tools. While the

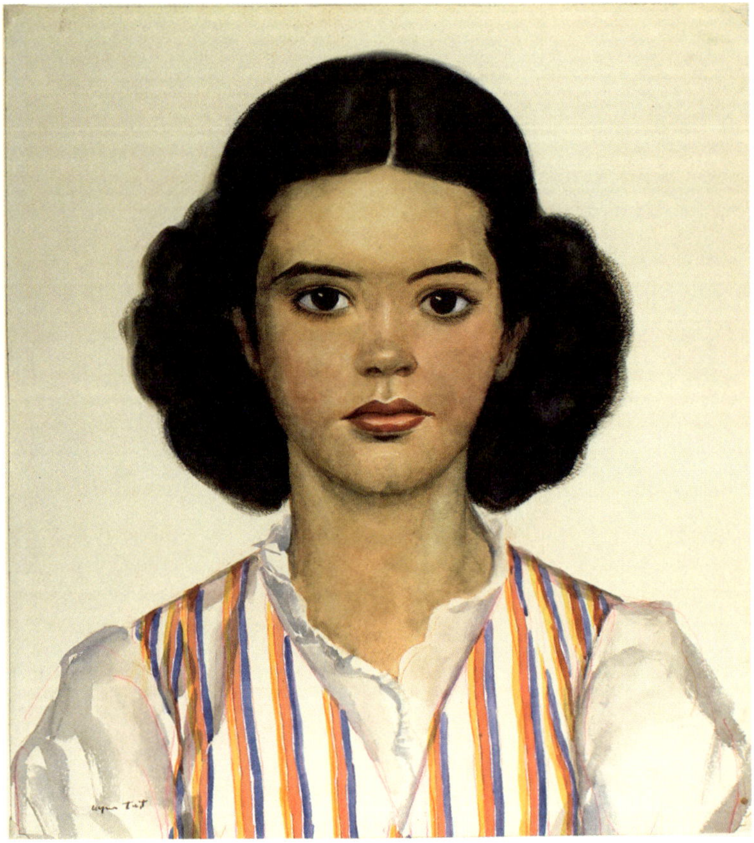

A watercolor portrait of Ann Baumann by Agnes Tait, n.d. Courtesy New Mexico Museum of Art,

New Mexico Museum of Art holds the world's largest collection of Baumann's work, the Baumann studio in the Palace Press is a "must see" for those interested in his printing process.

The New Mexico History Museum has benefited greatly from the generosity of the Ann Baumann Trust. Through its donations the museum's collection now includes a number of family domestic items, books, audio tapes, correspondence, and ephemera. That generosity also extends to the publication of this book, which could only have been realized with the solid support of the Trust.

In our search for additional works by artists represented in this book, we came across an entry in the Agnes Tait collection at the New Mexico Museum of Art titled "Ann Baumann." Our curiosity piqued, we asked to see what it could possibly be. What we found was a beautiful watercolor portrait of a teenage Ann, probably painted not long after Tait's arrival here in 1941. We wish Ann were here to tell us more stories of artists and holidays past.

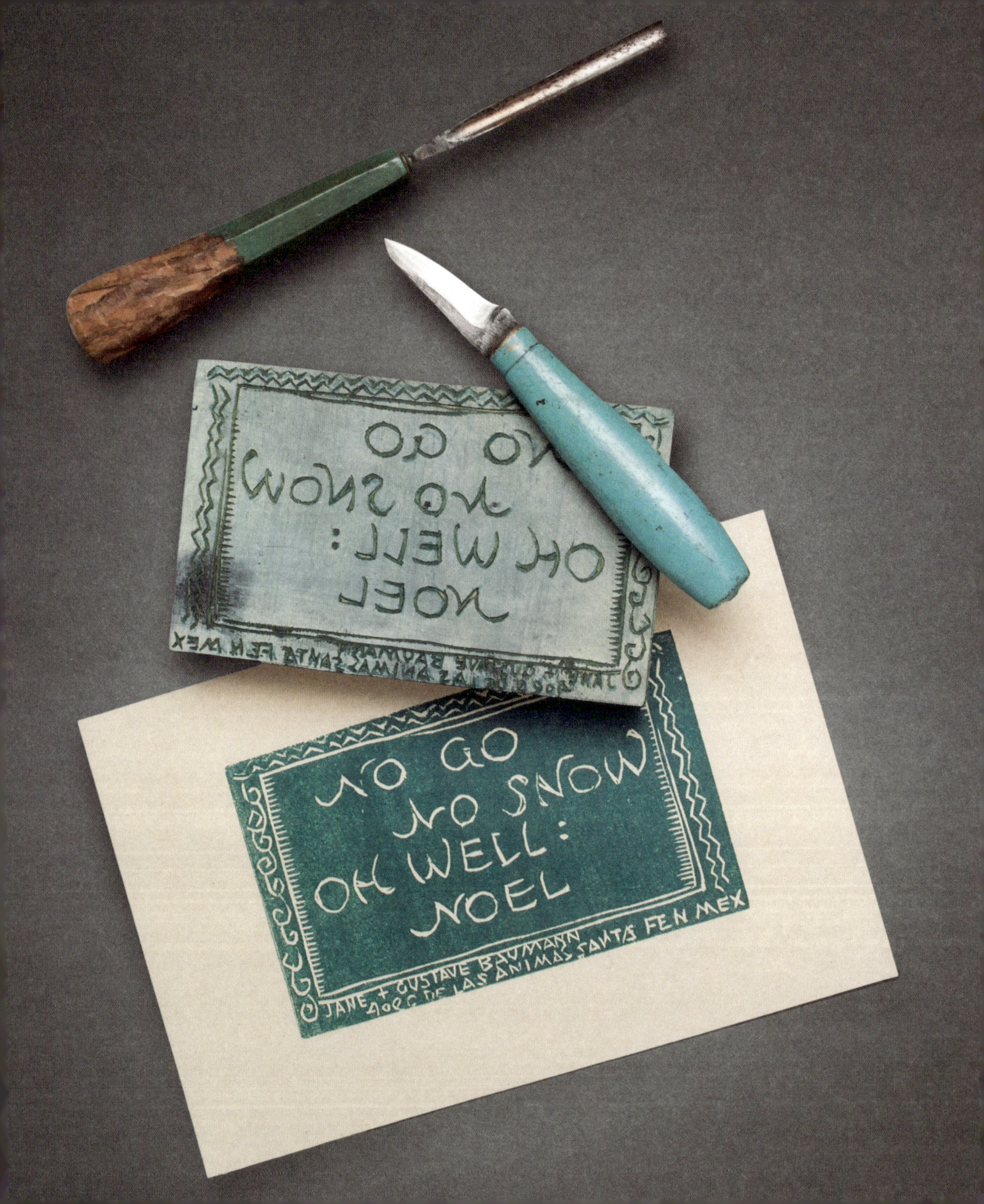
NO GO
NO SNOW
OH WELL:
NOEL
JANE + GUSTAVE BAUMANN
409 C DE LAS ANIMAS SANTA FE N MEX

Introduction

Jean Moss

The Baumanns — Gustave and Jane, and their daughter, Ann — were savers. They kept correspondence, examples of work, invoices, photographs, and the paper ephemera that accumulate in an artist's professional and domestic life. In the summer of 2012, the Fray Angélico Chávez History Library received several boxes of family archives from the Ann Baumann Trust. Included was a box of several hundred artist holiday cards. Many were cards received by the Baumanns from artist friends who lived in New Mexico, around the country, and overseas. There were also examples of the cards created by Baumann from his first days in Santa Fe until his death there in 1971. These were not commercially printed cards but small "editions" for friends and fellow artists, almost all hand printed, hand drawn, or hand colored.

No Go, No Snow—and no original cards with this design have been found. Did either Gus or Jane veto the idea of sending this card? Or perhaps it snowed, after all! The proof was made at the Palace Press.

Like any collection, this one contains holes, mysteries, and puzzles. It is almost second nature for artists to try their hand at "homemade" cards, yet some noted artists are conspicuous by their absence. Were they philosophically opposed, or just saw no need to spend their time and energy in this form of communication? Perhaps some sent commercial cards. We know that some even created commercial cards as a means of earning money. Baumann consistently created holiday cards that were anticipated and prized. For this book we have called on other institutions and generous lenders to fill some of the gaps, and we hope the attention that comes to the collection will inspire readers to check in old trunks and shoeboxes for forgotten gems.

Gustave Baumann was born in Germany and immigrated with his family to Chicago at the age of ten. At sixteen he left school to work in commercial art houses by day and attend classes at the Art Institute of Chicago by night. He saved enough to study art in Germany for a year, and on his return to America began balancing commercial work with fine art. A period of years spent between Chicago and the artist colony of Brown County, Indiana, saw the beginning of his mastery of color woodblock printing.

In the autumn of 1918, Baumann arrived in Santa Fe, a quiet town of about six thousand people, with adobe houses lining narrow, unpaved streets. Situated in the clear air of the Sangre de Cristo Mountains, Santa Fe, like Taos, its neighbor to the north, was beginning to draw artists from other parts of the country. The new Museum of Fine Arts made a conscious

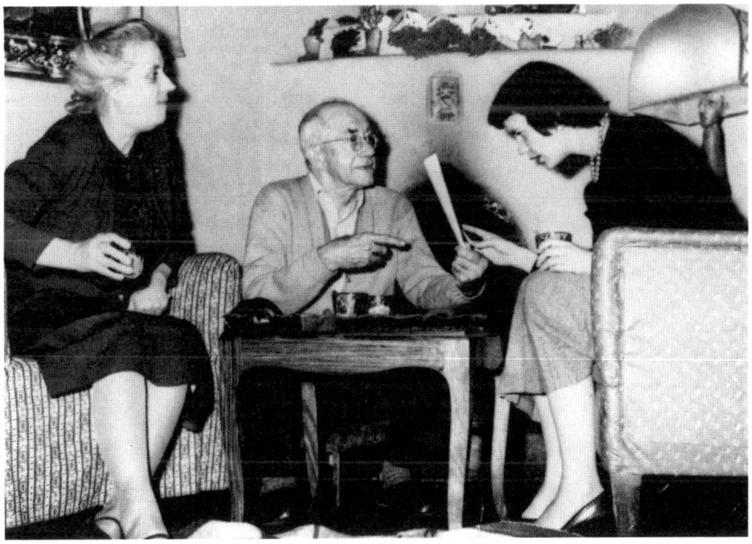

Home for the Holidays. The Baumann family gathered in their living room at Christmas, 1954. When this photo was taken, Ann was twenty-seven years old and in living in California. Photographer unknown.

effort to attract and support serious artists, and Baumann set up a studio in the basement of the museum. After trying out three other locations, 1923 found him constructing a house designed to create a complete artistic milieu in which he could live and work. At a San Felipe Pueblo Christmas dance that year he met Jane Devereux Henderson, a classically trained actress and opera singer from Denver. They married in 1925 and two years later their only child, Ann, was born. The small family became an integral part of a thriving community of artists, writers, and intellectuals.

Artists and writers came to Santa Fe for many reasons. Some were disenchanted with the rigidness and exclusiveness of the eastern art establishment or sought to escape large, noisy cities. With access to Europe cut off by war, others came from art colonies like Provincetown and Carmel to investigate a new art scene. They were attracted by the quality of light, by the picturesque landscape, the adobe buildings, the ritual and formality of the Hispanic culture, and the ancient, persistent tradition of the Pueblo Indians. Many hoped to find creative energy in a simpler life. More than a few came for health reasons and, charmed, stayed. But almost all who came, even those who came only in summer, became productive, involved members of their community.

Most of the artists and writers were poor, and they worked hard, spending long days painting or writing. But that didn't stop them having fun. They formed community theatres, a chamber music group which included a percussion section of pots and pans, and lived the bohemian life with parties and fierce intellectual and artistic discussions. During prohibition, many made their own spirits, and the stories of dodging U.S. Revenue officers caused both apprehension and merriment.

They invigorated the annual Santa Fe Fiesta, which had been for a couple hundred years purely a religious commemora-

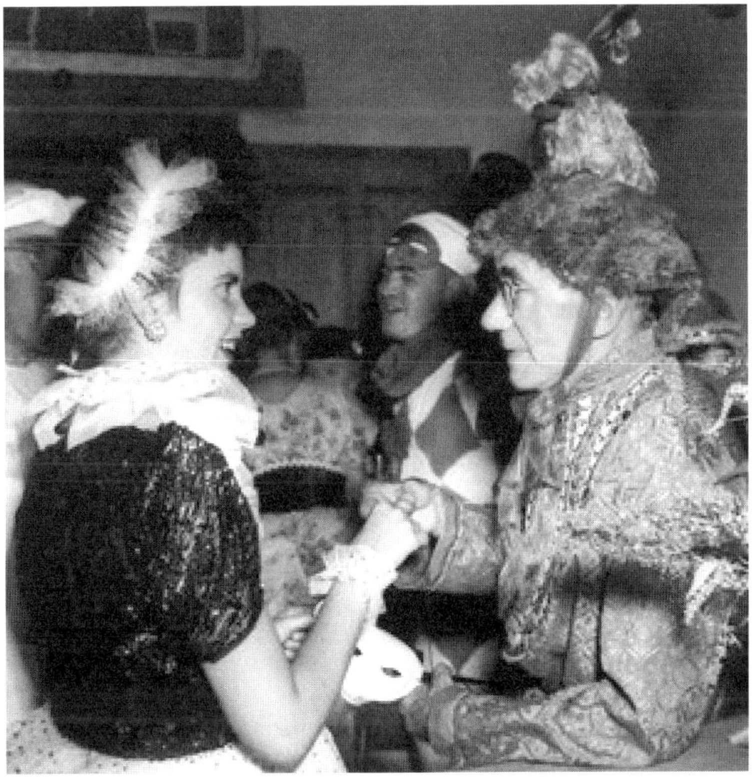

Ann and Gustave Baumann at a costume party, August 1949.

tion. In 1917, a group of artists and writers decided to make fiesta a true party and dressed up in Spanish, cowboy, and Indian costumes. As the years went by, fiesta expanded to include several parades. In 1926, Will Shuster and Gus Baumann created the burning of the giant papier mâché puppet Zozobra (Old Man Gloom) to inaugurate the festivities.

The artist community was active in war work in both the First and Second World Wars. The Santa Fe Players for many years donated proceeds to the Red Cross. During a bad drought in the twenties, artists wrote and produced plays at the Museum of Fine Arts to provide relief for the Indian Pueblos, establish a milk fund for children, and buy feed for cattle. A number of artists were involved in conservation work for the local churches. Baumann, in fact, spent a month conserving "La Conquistadora," a wooden figure of the Virgin brought to Santa Fe by Spanish colonists in 1625. Artist societies were formed in Taos and Santa Fe, and the two communities retained strong bonds.

All was not idyllic, of course. There were divorces and problems with alcoholism; there were jealousies, rivalries, and petty quarrels. There was the constant struggle of the artists to improve their craft. Especially during the Depression years there was the problem of income, some of which was supplemented by work for the New Deal art programs. And like the rest of the country, they lost friends and family in the two world wars.

Gustave Baumann and his artist friends who were involved in the community and art scenes of Taos and Santa Fe contributed much to placing this "backwater region" in the nation's artistic consciousness. While they might not recognize today what their quiet little towns have become, the memory and spirit of the times captured in their holiday greetings remain.

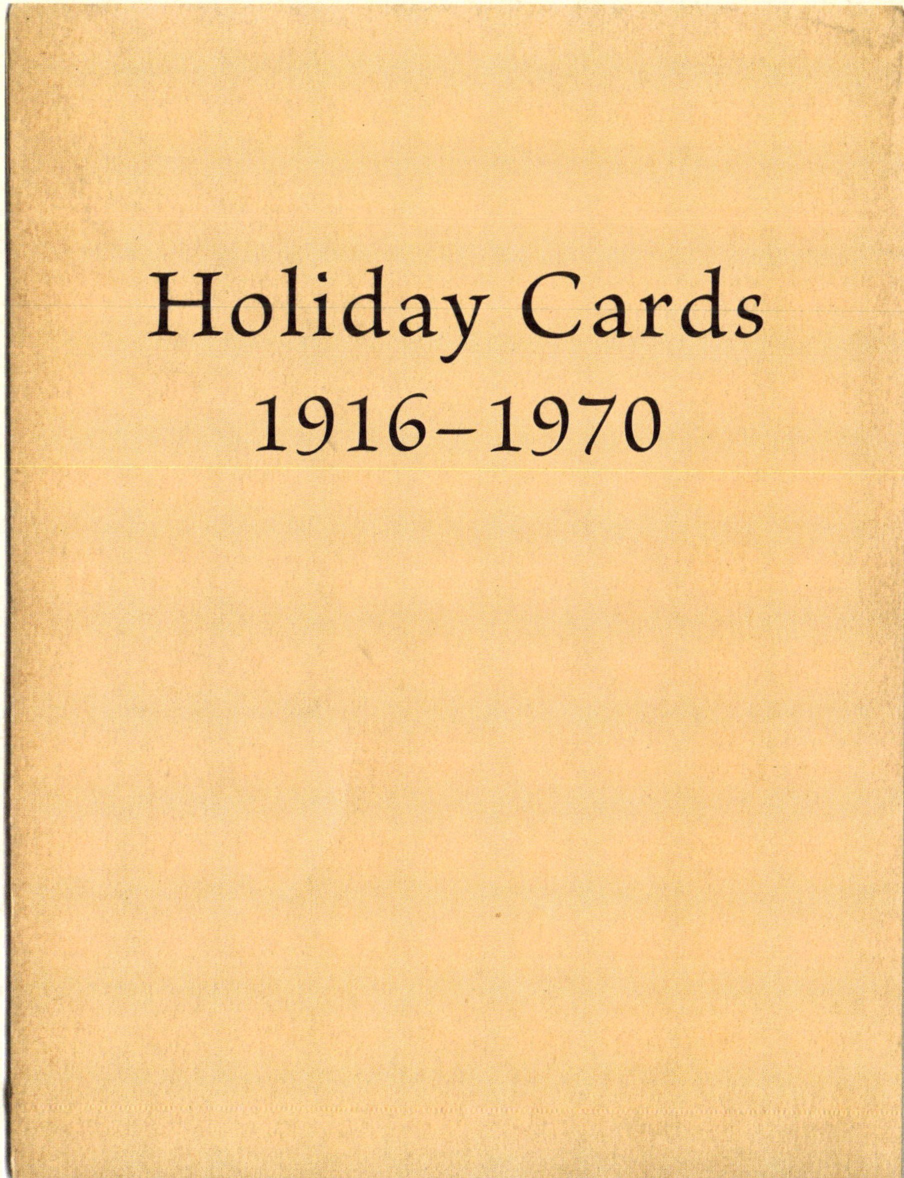
Holiday Cards
1916–1970

The stage is set as New Mexico becomes the 47th State in 1912. Its centuries-old native and Hispanic cultures had already been "discovered" by artists, archaeologists, and anthropologists. Now, for the first time, American tourists can experience the "ancient and exotic" without leaving the boundaries of the country—all from the relative comfort of trains and automobiles.

GUSTAVE BAUMANN.
TWO-COLOR WOODCUT. 1919

Baumann sends his first greeting card with a western theme—he gets it all—cowboys and Indians! He also uses his Koshare Press logo on the back of the card. The Koshare are sacred clowns and tricksters that appear in Pueblo religious ceremony. Baumann was very attracted to the Koshare for their sense of humor and worldview, which fell right in line with his.

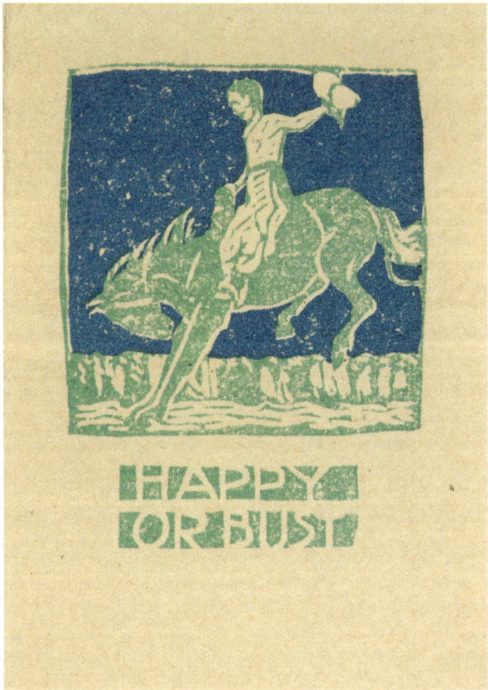

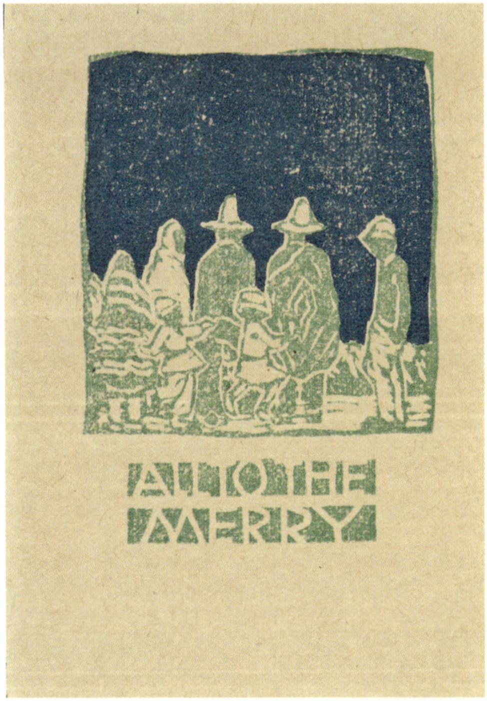

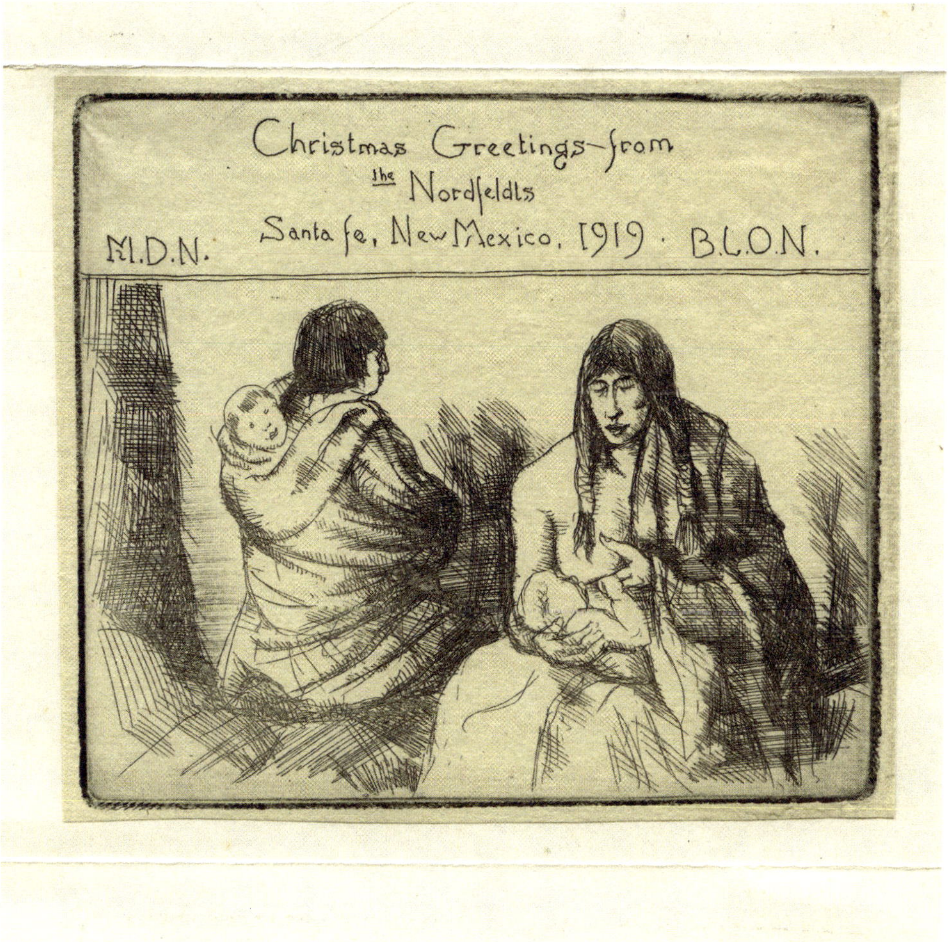

B. J. O. NORDFELDT. ETCHING. 1919

Newly arrived in Santa Fe, Baumann's old friend from Chicago and Provincetown, B. J. O. Nordfeldt, uses this scene of a nursing Native American woman as a lovely reference to the Madonna and child. Even an experienced printmaker like Nordfeldt couldn't avoid making a "rookie mistake," here reversing the "J" in his own initials. Swedish-born Nordfeldt and German-born Baumann were close in age and arrived in the United States at about the same time, both apprenticing in commercial printing houses in Chicago.

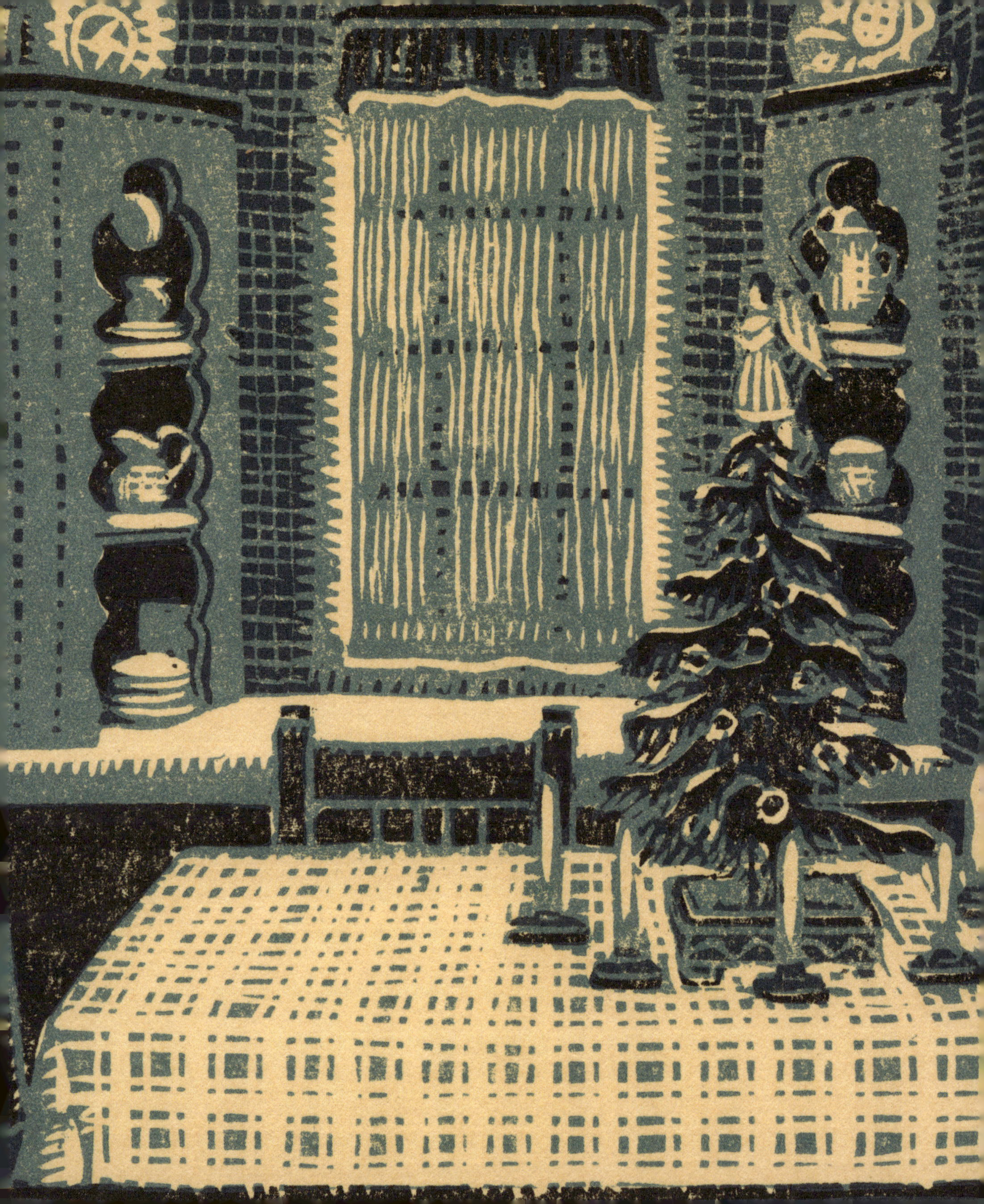

The decade of the 1920s began on a high note. The Great War was behind us. Artists were returning with expanded worldviews and finding solace and peace in the Southwest. No one could foresee the coming crash of October 1929.

GUSTAVE BAUMANN. WOODCUT. 1921

Baumann creates a wonderful card using the Pueblo Indian deer dance as his theme. The deer dance is performed in most of the pueblos around Christmas and New Year. Baumann, like most of the Santa Fe and Taos artists, attended Indian dances and feast days, and these are the subjects of many of his prints.

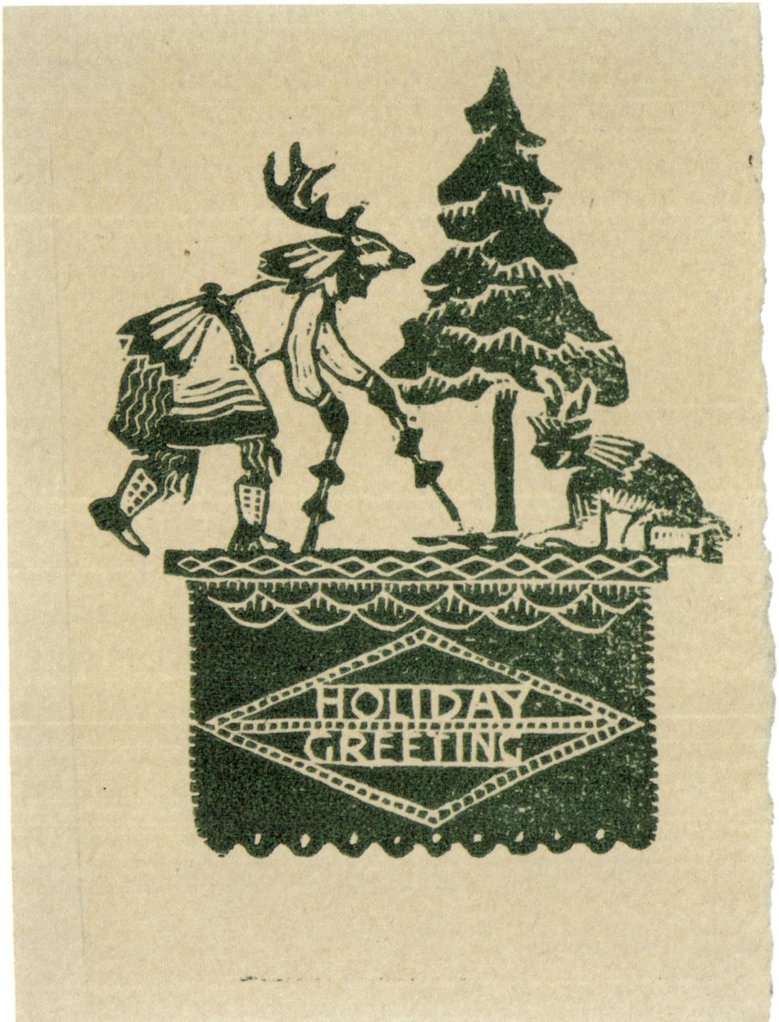

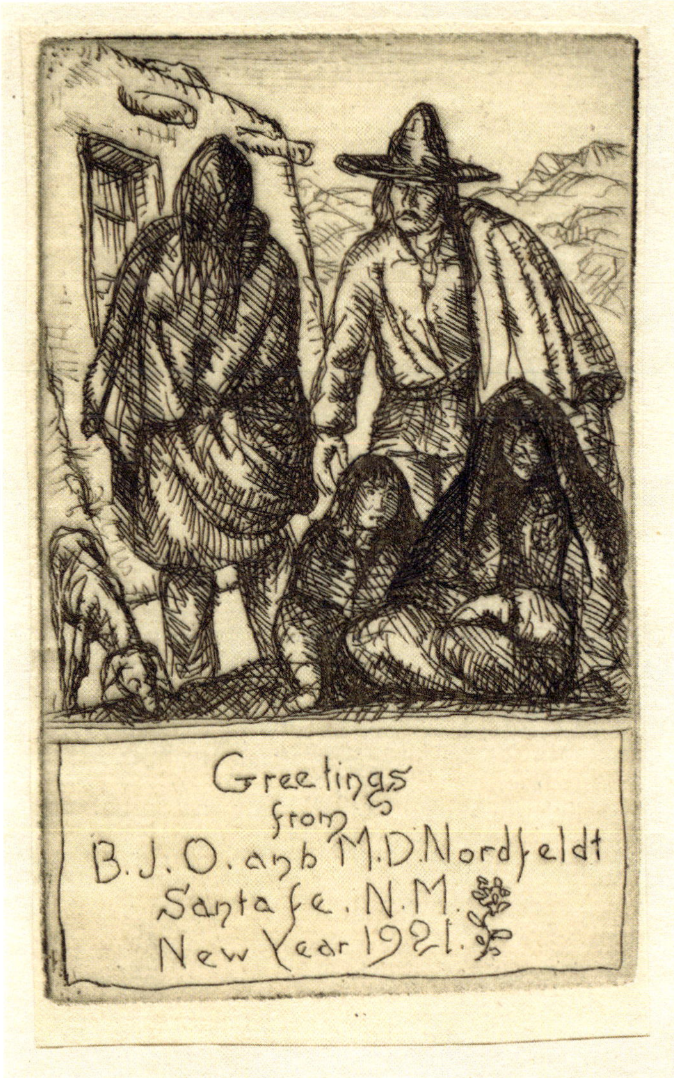

B. J. O. NORDFELDT. ETCHING. 1921

Nordfeldt usually chose subjects with emotional power, as is evidenced in the Hispanic family scene he uses for this 1921 New Year's card. Nordfeldt's prints were his primary source of income until 1926 when he turned exclusively to painting.

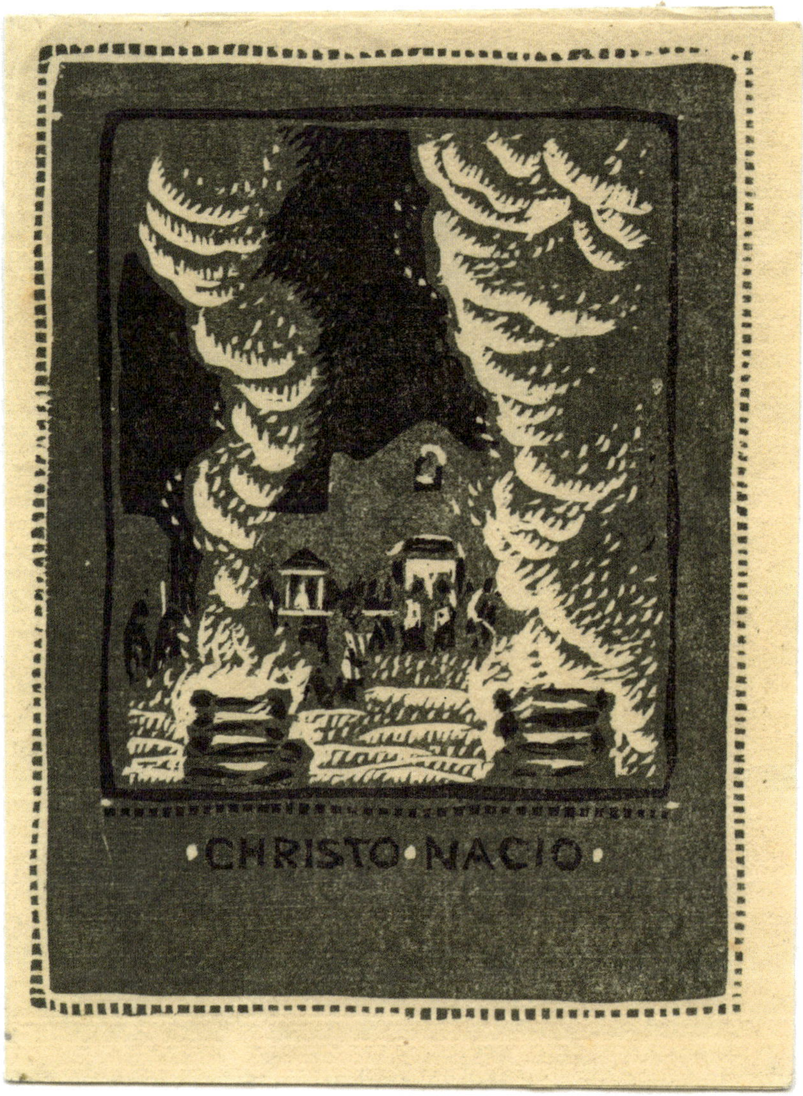

GUSTAVE BAUMANN. TWO-COLOR WOODCUT. 1922

Baumann sends a holiday card with a traditional Hispanic theme. The Koshare Press logo is on the back of the card.

GUSTAVE BAUMANN. TWO-COLOR WOODCUT. 1923

Burros still wandered the streets in 1923. Firewood vendors brought their wares by burro to Burro Alley near the plaza, and it was common to see burros tethered in back yards. Chile then, as now, was a staple on dining tables, and *ristras* of chile hung drying from the eaves. For a young man from the big city of Chicago, it was truly the "land of mañana."

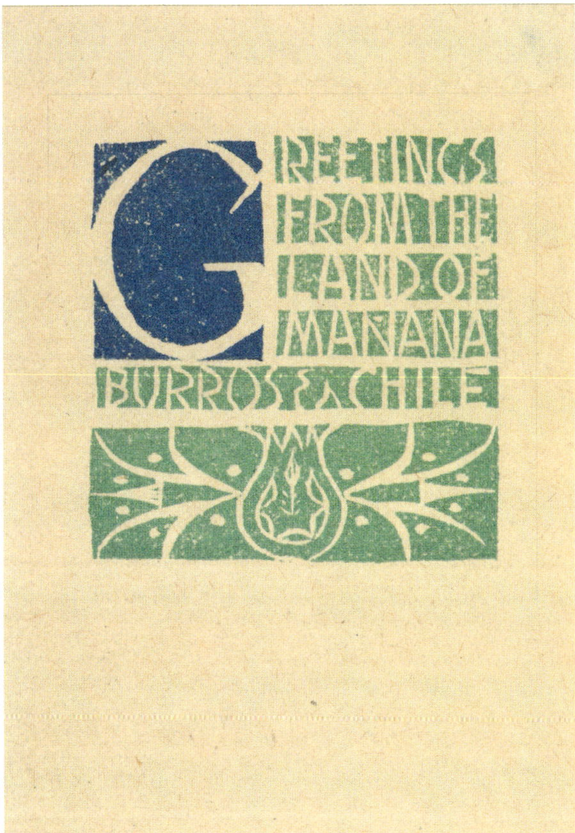

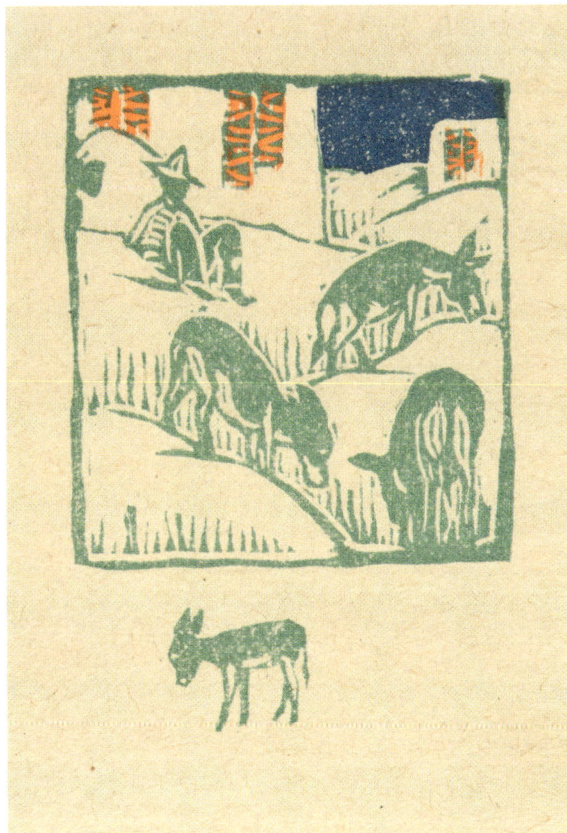

GUSTAVE BAUMANN. WOODCUT. 1924

Baumann's last card as a bachelor greets the 1925 New Year. This vivid impression was made on a rare Chinese paper, while other impressions from the same block exist on bright pink and deep teal papers. Throughout his career as an artist, Baumann kept a variety of unusual decorative papers that often were used for his holiday cards.

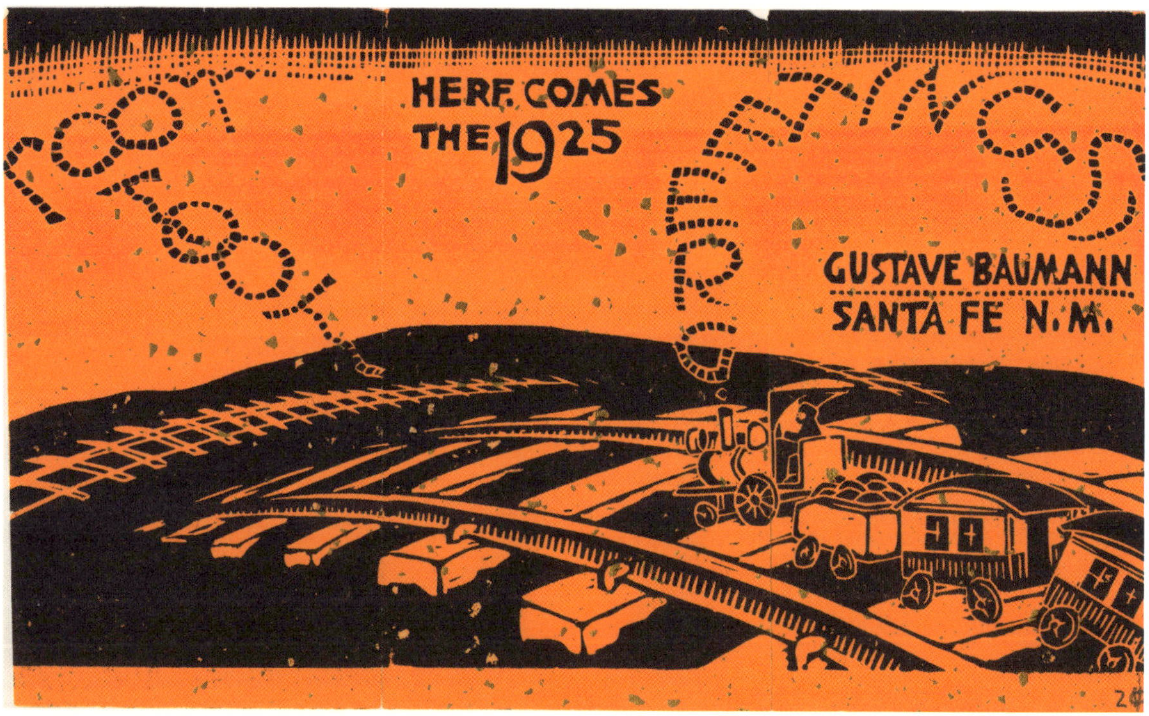

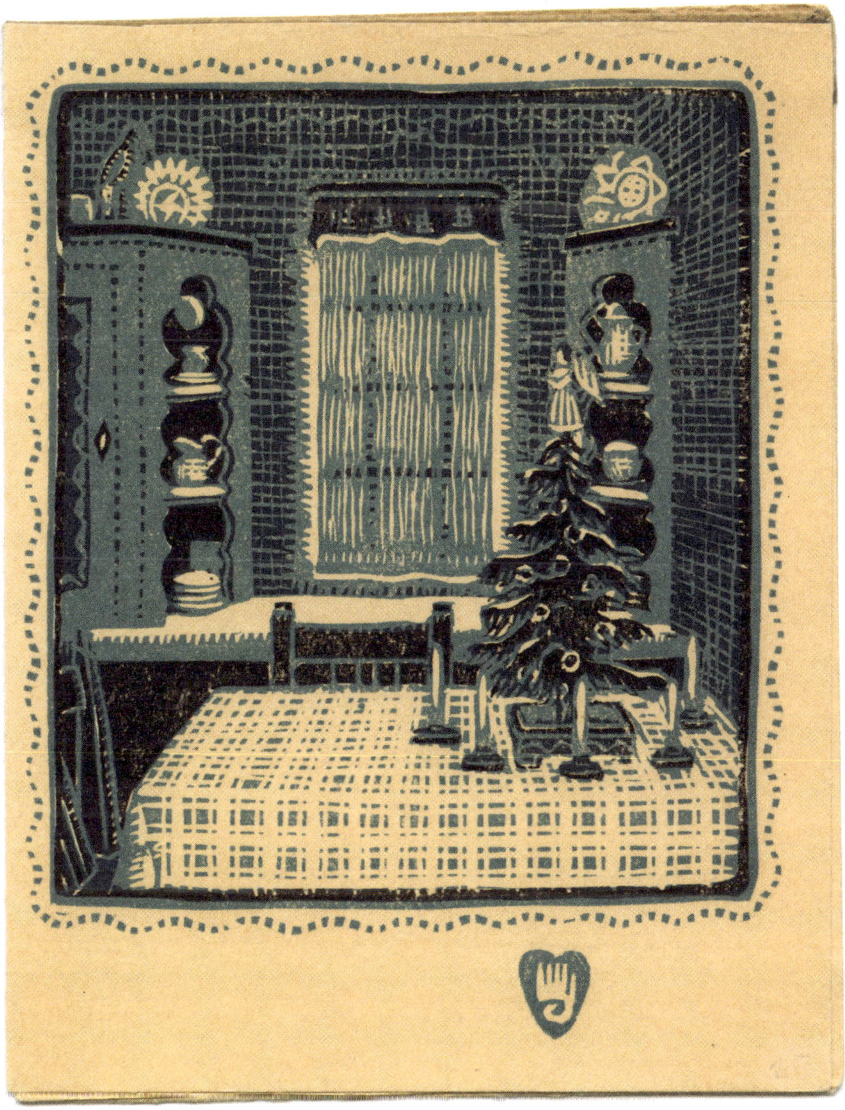

GUSTAVE BAUMANN. TWO-COLOR WOODCUT. 1925

Jane and Gus, newly married, send their first holiday card together, showing the dining room of their house decorated for the holidays.

ERNEST BLUMENSCHEIN.
PHOTO-ENGRAVING FROM
ORIGINAL PEN-AND-INK. 1925

"Blumy" greets the New Year with comical portraits of the family—he, with his paint-laden palette and crooked halo, and his wife Mary and sixteen-year-old daughter Helen in their holiday finery with their halos intact. Ernest, one of the founders of the Taos Society of Artists, was the patriarch of an artistic family. His wife was a successful painter and illustrator, and his daughter also became a painter and printmaker.

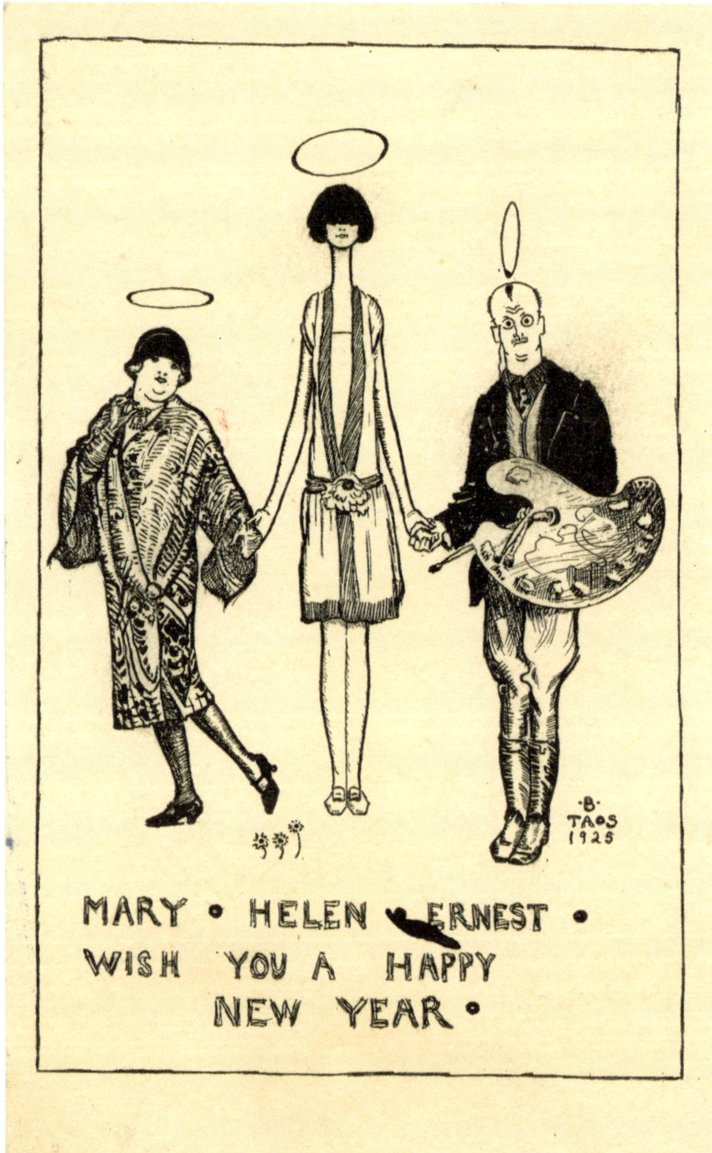

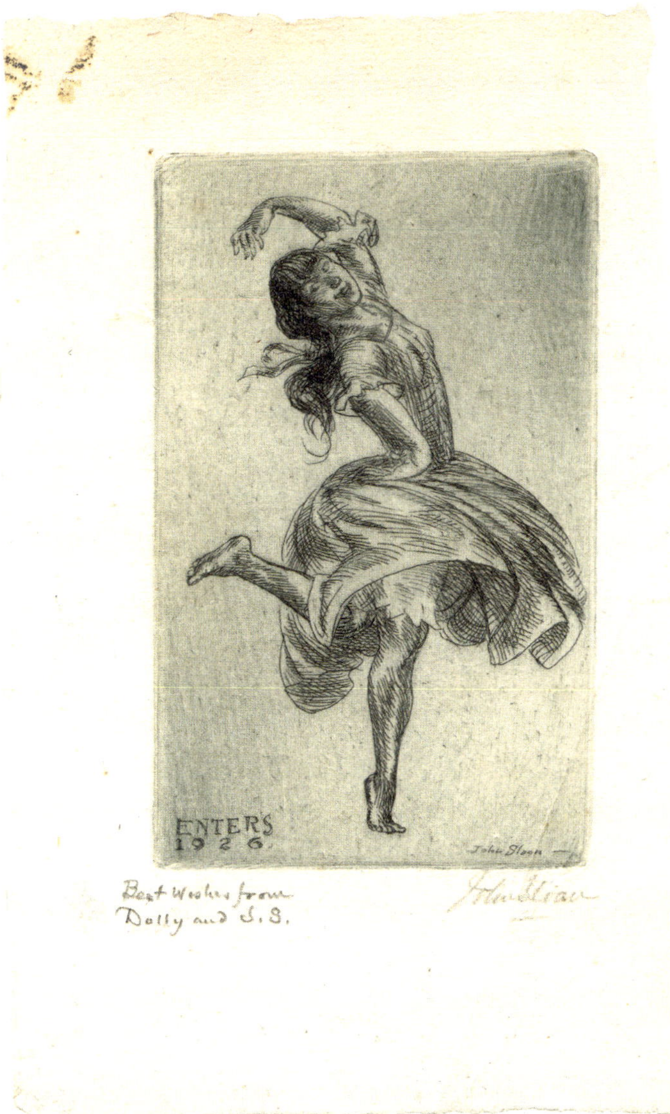

JOHN SLOAN. ETCHING. 1926

Sloan sends a joyous dancer to welcome the New Year. John and his wife, Dolly, were close friends of the Baumanns. Both couples were involved in the Santa Fe Players, where John and Gus worked on sets and lighting and Jane and Dolly often appeared on stage.

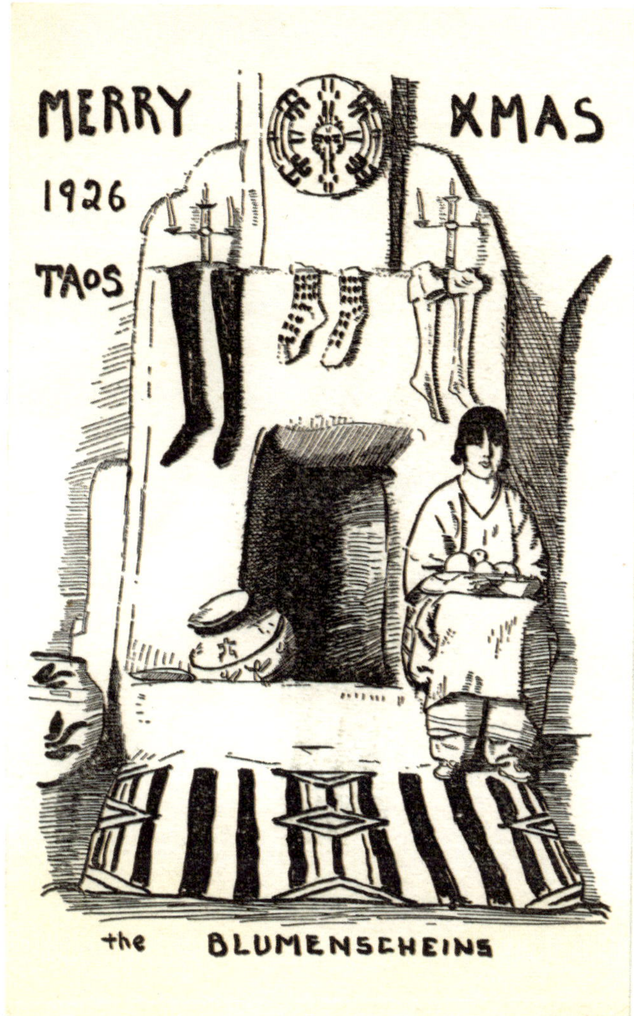

MARY GREENE BLUMENSCHEIN. PHOTO-ENGRAVING FROM ORIGINAL PEN-AND-INK. 1926

Mary Blumenschein portrays her daughter, Helen, dressed in Pueblo costume, waiting for Santa Claus before the ubiquitous kiva fireplace displaying the family stockings.

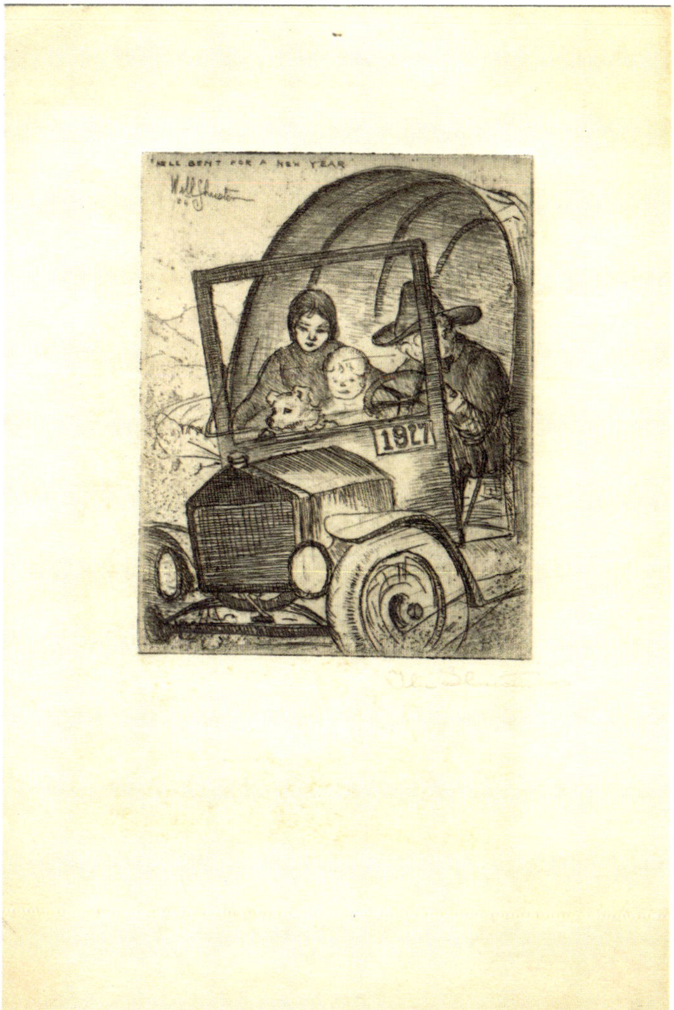

WILL SHUSTER. ETCHING. 1926

Shuster and his small family drive their trademark "covered wagon" into 1927. Fashioned from a Model T touring car, it had a utilitarian use for sketching and camping trips and appeared in local parades with a papier-mâché horse attached to the hood that appeared to be pulling the wagon.

GUSTAVE BAUMANN. WOODCUT. 1927

This bird's-eye view of the Baumann home on E. Buena Vista Road (now Camino de las Animas) announces that "the wild and little known . . . province" of artists and Indians has been domesticated.

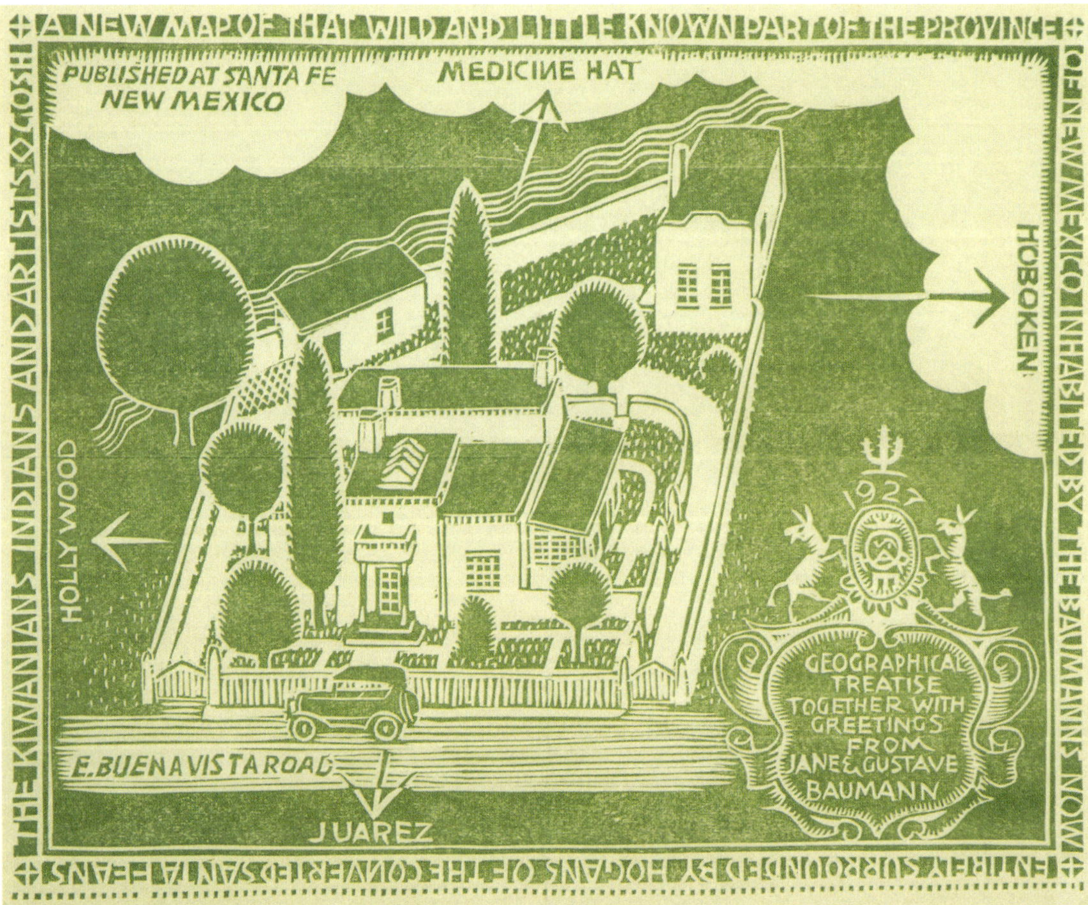

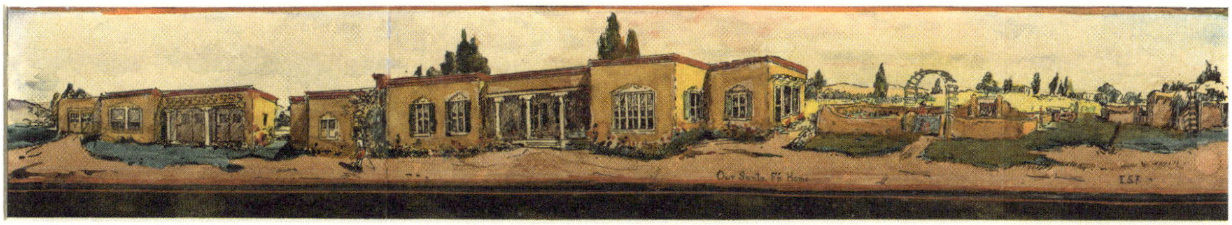

EVA SCOTT FÉNYES. WATERCOLOR. 1927

Fényes, a wealthy, creative woman and an integral part of the intellectual community of Santa Fe, uses a watercolor rendering of the newly finished house she designed as a holiday card.

GERALD CASSIDY. WOODCUT WITH HAND COLORING. 1927

Gerald and Ina Cassidy celebrate Christmas of 1927 by returning to their Santa Fe home. They had been traveling in Europe, where Gerald had considerable artistic success, but they were obviously happy to return to "home sweet home."

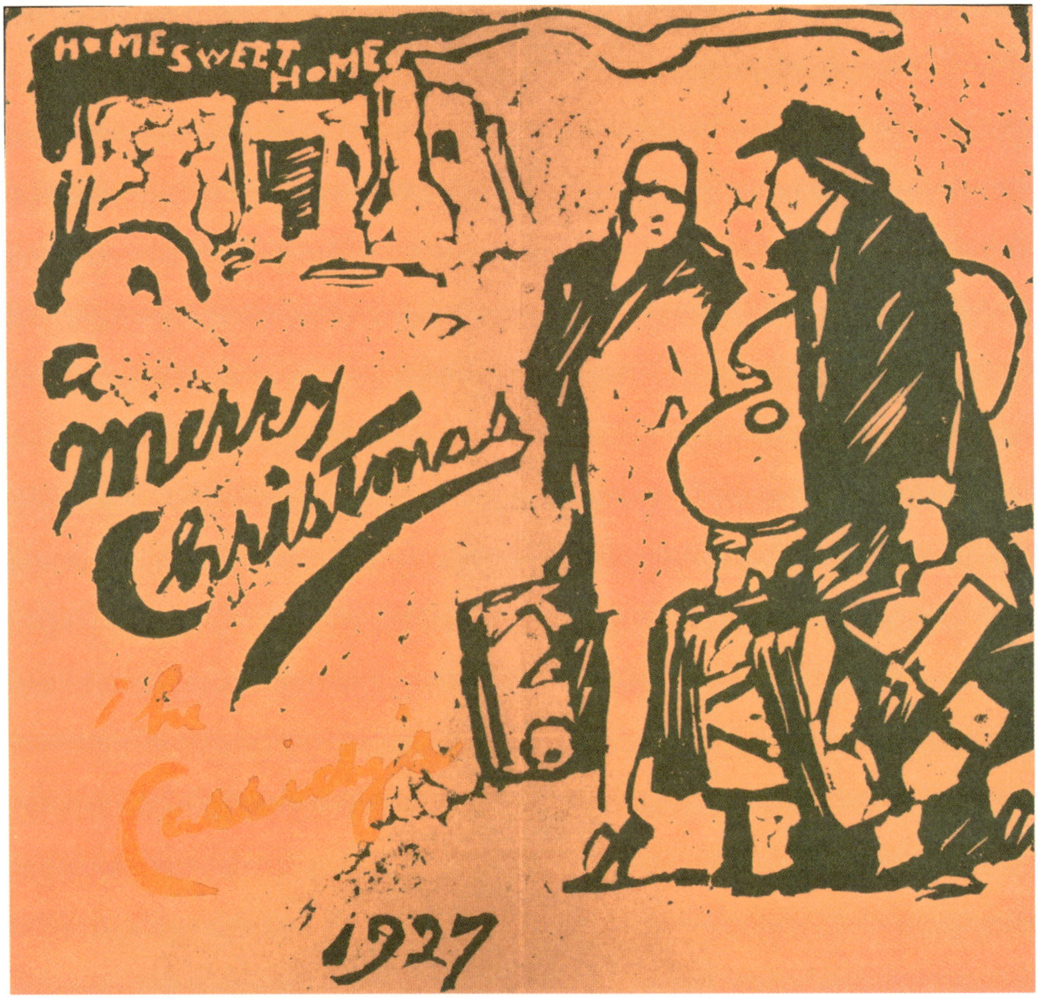

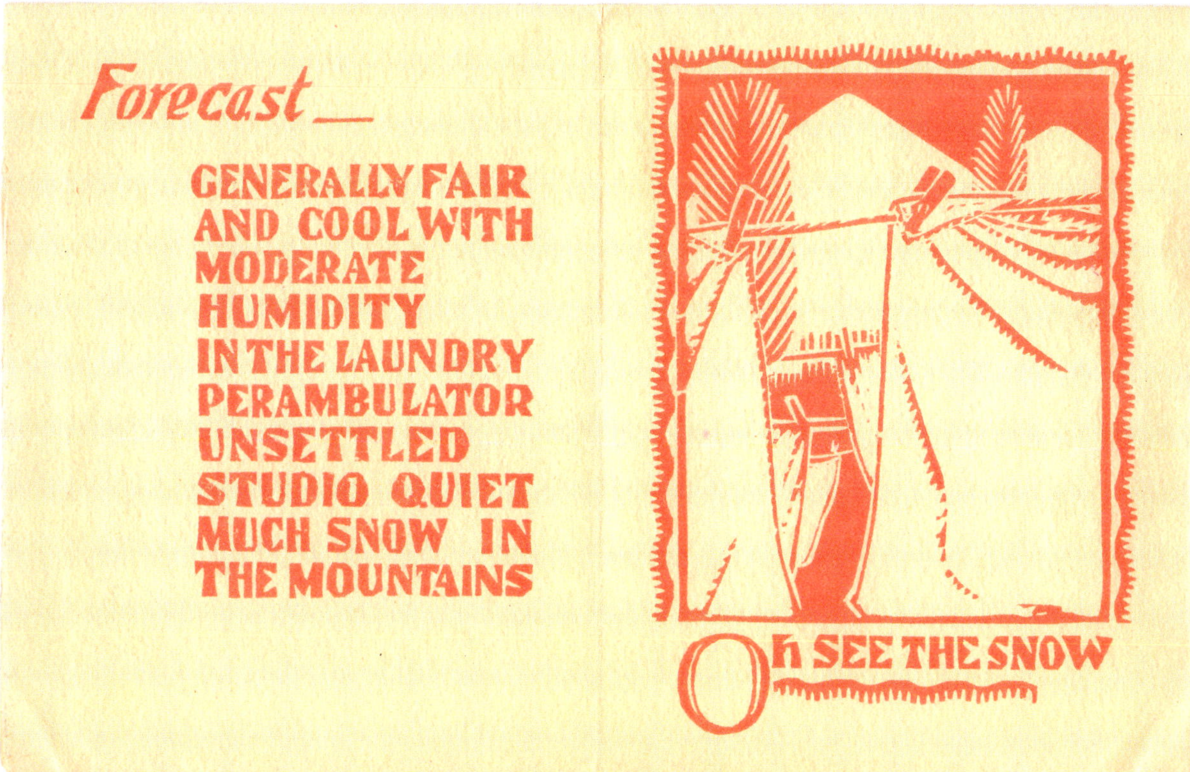

GUSTAVE BAUMANN. COLOR WOODCUT. 1928

Snow is forecast for 1928. Daughter Ann was born in 1927, and the forecast includes "snow white" diapers along with the snowy mountains.

WILL SHUSTER. ETCHING. 1928

It's 1928, the year before the stock market crash and the beginning of the Great Depression. Will Shuster, his family, and pets are sitting on top of the world.

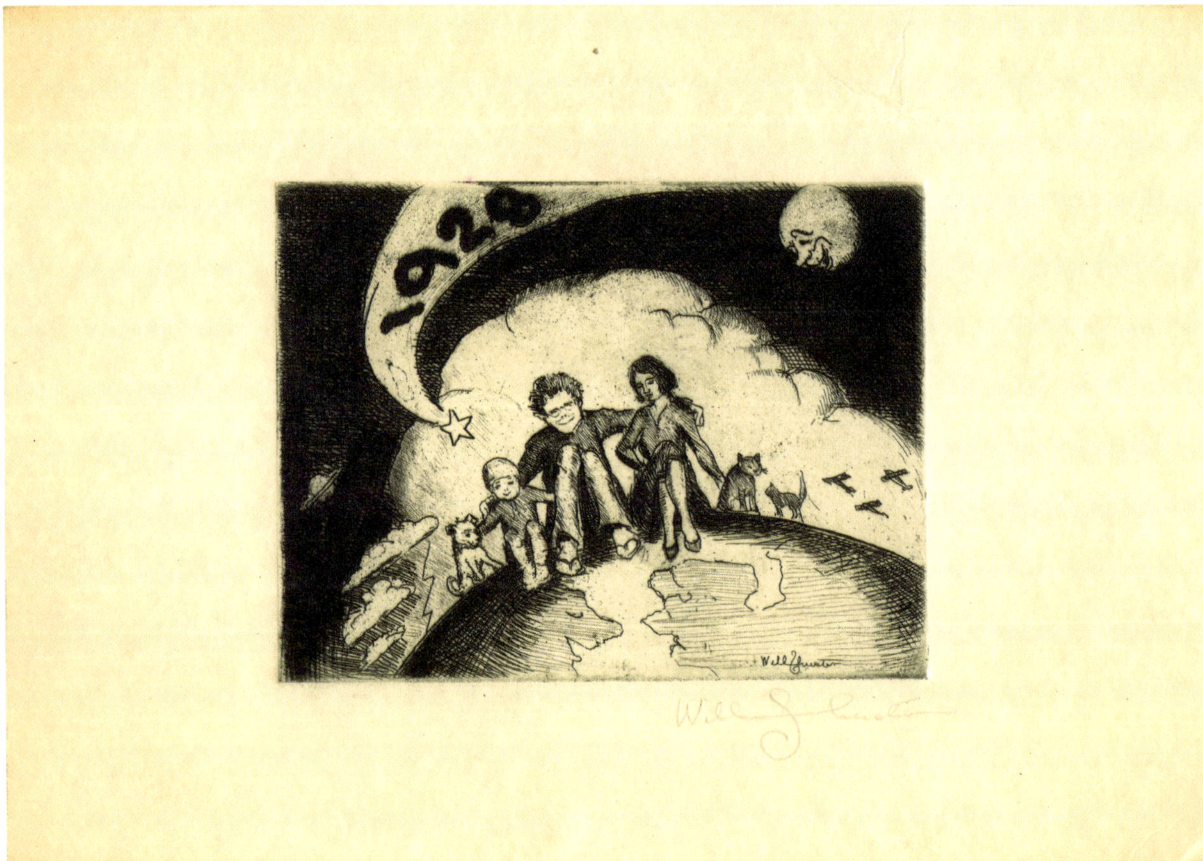

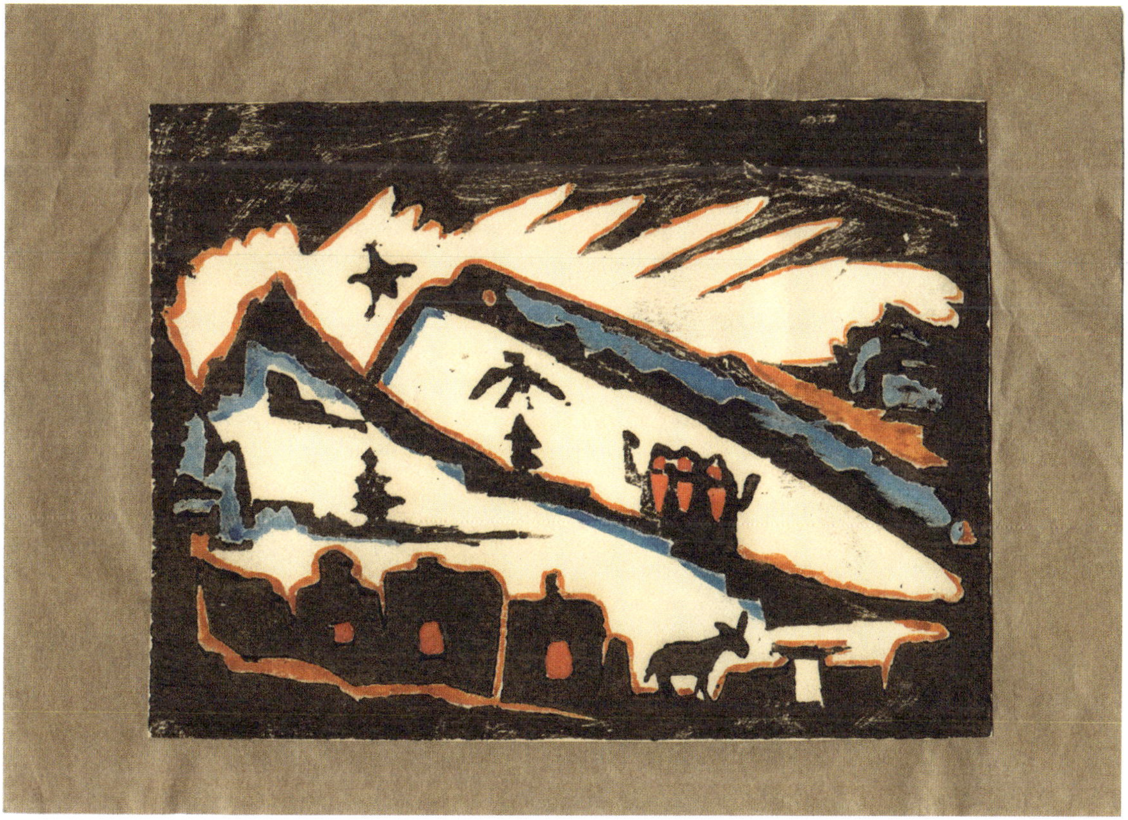

FRANK APPLEGATE. HAND-COLORED WOODCUT. 1920S

Even with a minimum of recognizable imagery, this card says "New Mexico." Applegate, a painter and sculptor, also tried his hand at printmaking. This print, titled *Mountain Side,* appeared in Spud Johnson's literary journal *Laughing Horse* in August 1925.

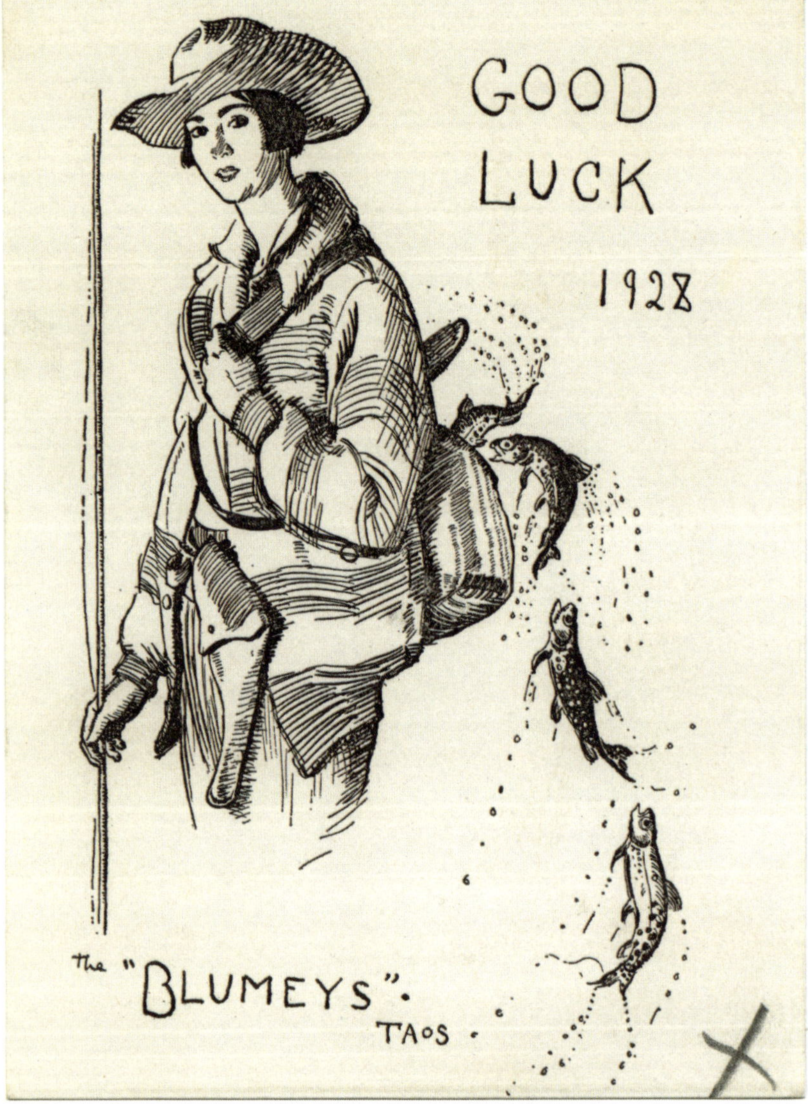

MARY GREENE BLUMENSCHEIN. PHOTO-ENGRAVING FROM ORIGINAL PEN-AND-INK. 1928

The Blumenscheins offer good luck for all in the coming year with an illustration of fish jumping into the creel of their daughter Helen, an avid fisherwoman.

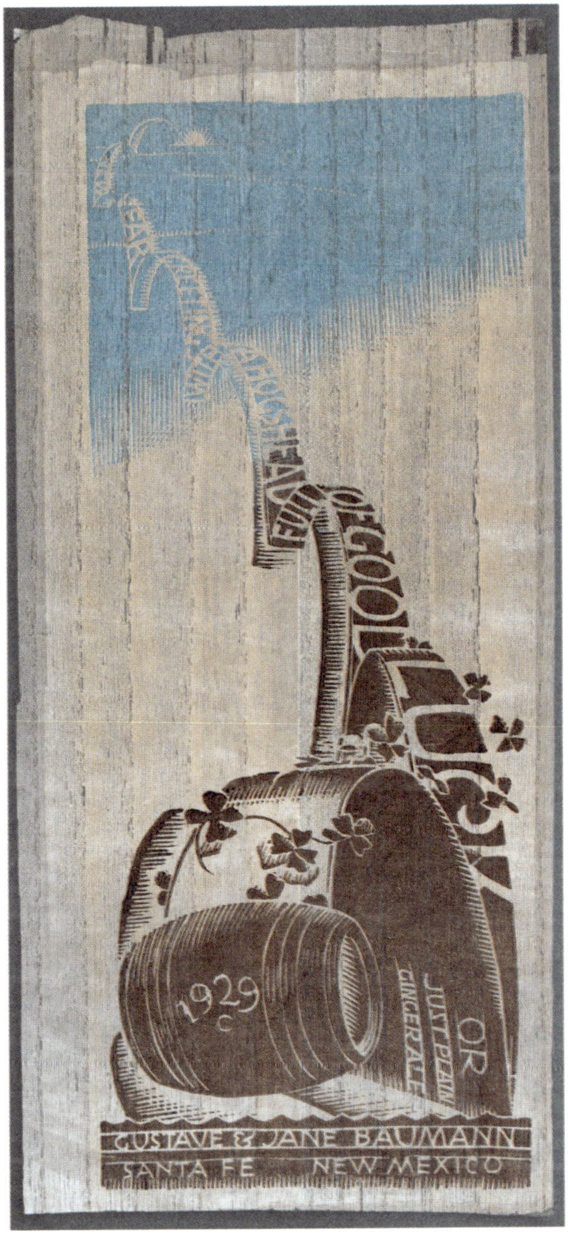

GUSTAVE BAUMANN.
COLOR WOODCUT. 1929

The bouncing barrel sends a message of optimism for the next year and implies a good one past. Although Prohibition remained the law of the land until 1933, this may be a hint that the barrel is full of something other than ginger ale. The card shown here is printed on Japanese wood veneer, with a single block inked in two colors.

The Great Depression dragged slowly through the decade of the 1930s, greatly affecting the art colonies. When there is little money, it goes for food—not art. Luckily, work on various New Deal art projects afforded some gainful employment for many New Mexico artists.

GUSTAVE BAUMANN. WOODCUT. 1930

Ennui in Valhalla refers to Witter Bynner's play *Cake*, which was the social event of 1929 in Santa Fe. The central character of the play is a very bored, very wealthy woman loosely based on Mabel Dodge Lujan. A painting of this languorous scene by Russell Cheney is in the Albuquerque Museum.

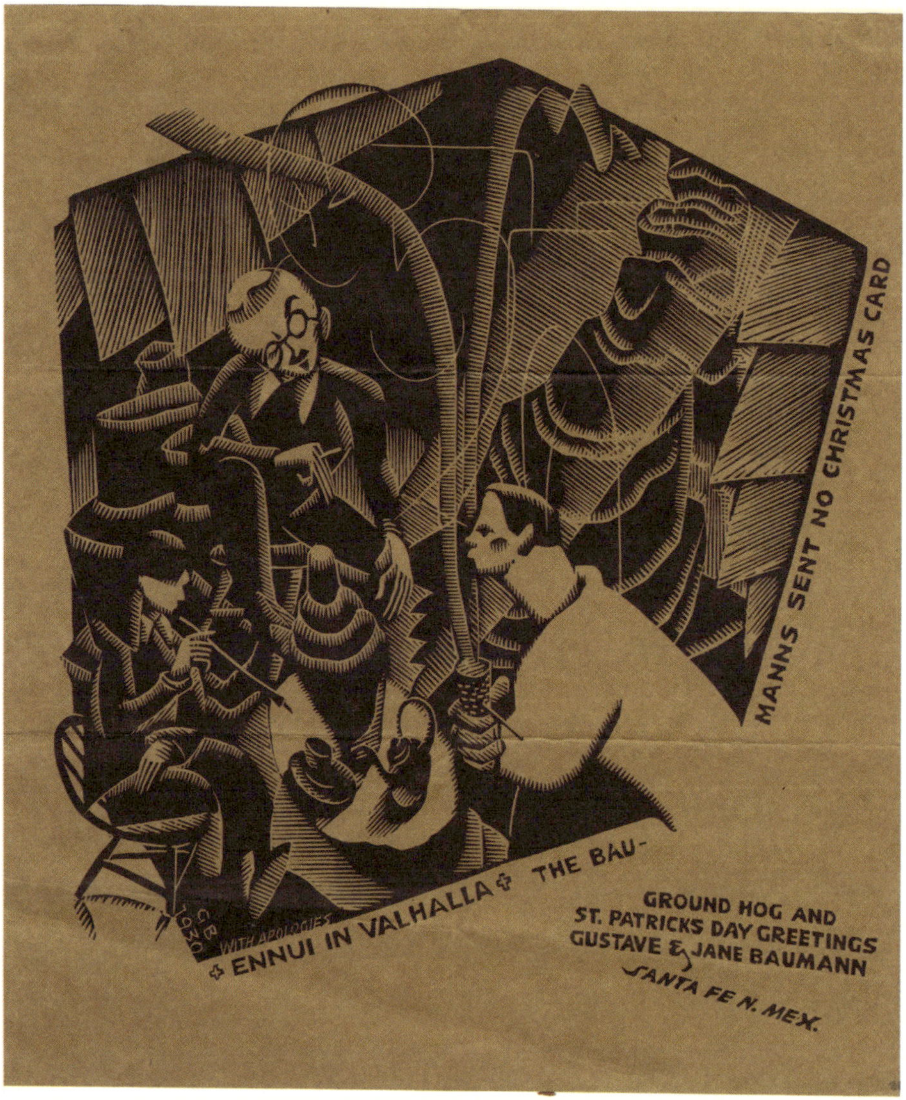

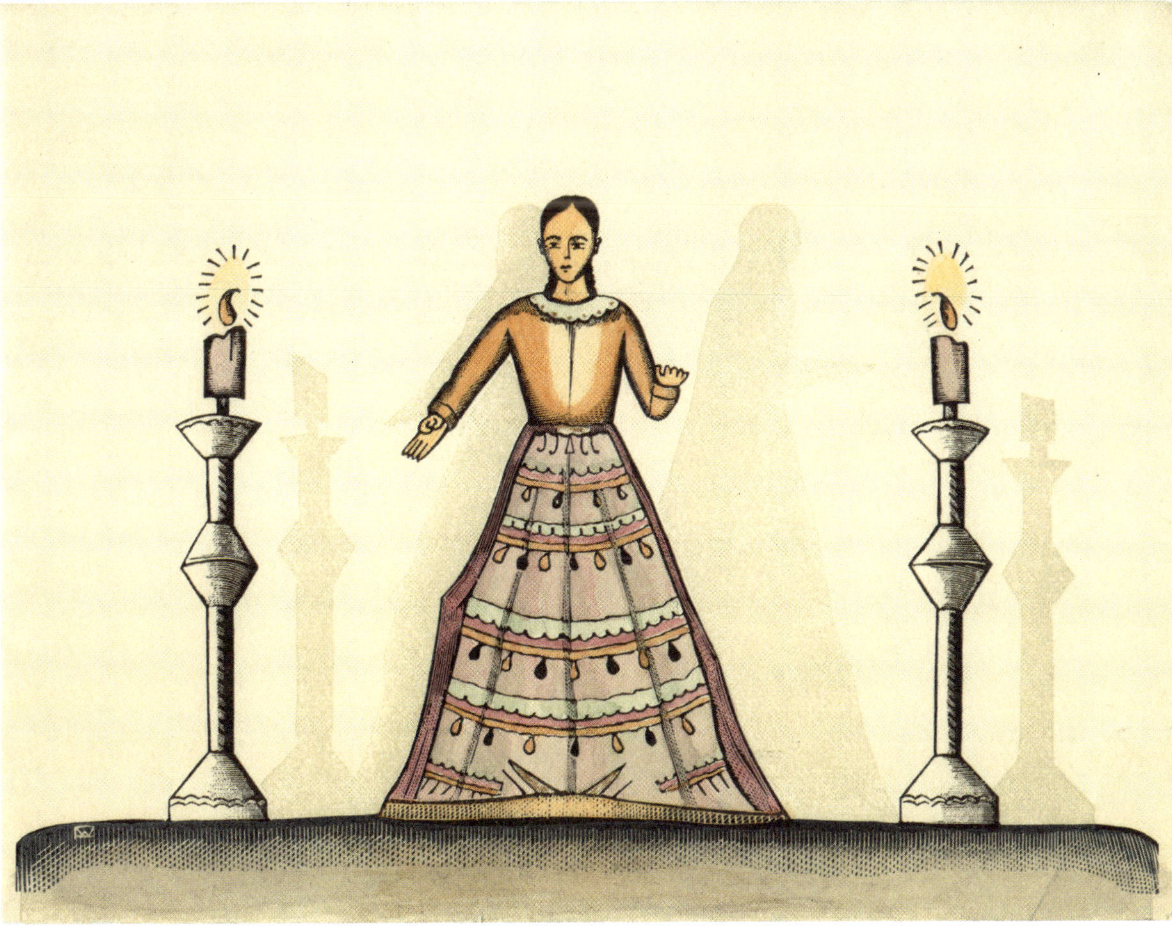

WILLARD CLARK. TWO-COLOR WOODCUT WITH HAND COLORING. UNDATED, CA. 1930S

The bulto, bordered by tin candlesticks, reflects Clark's interest in Hispanic Santa Fe. Clark, who was raised in South America, was fluent in Spanish and felt completely at home in Northern New Mexico. Almost all of Clark's work, including the commercial, contains elements relating to the Hispanic culture of New Mexico.

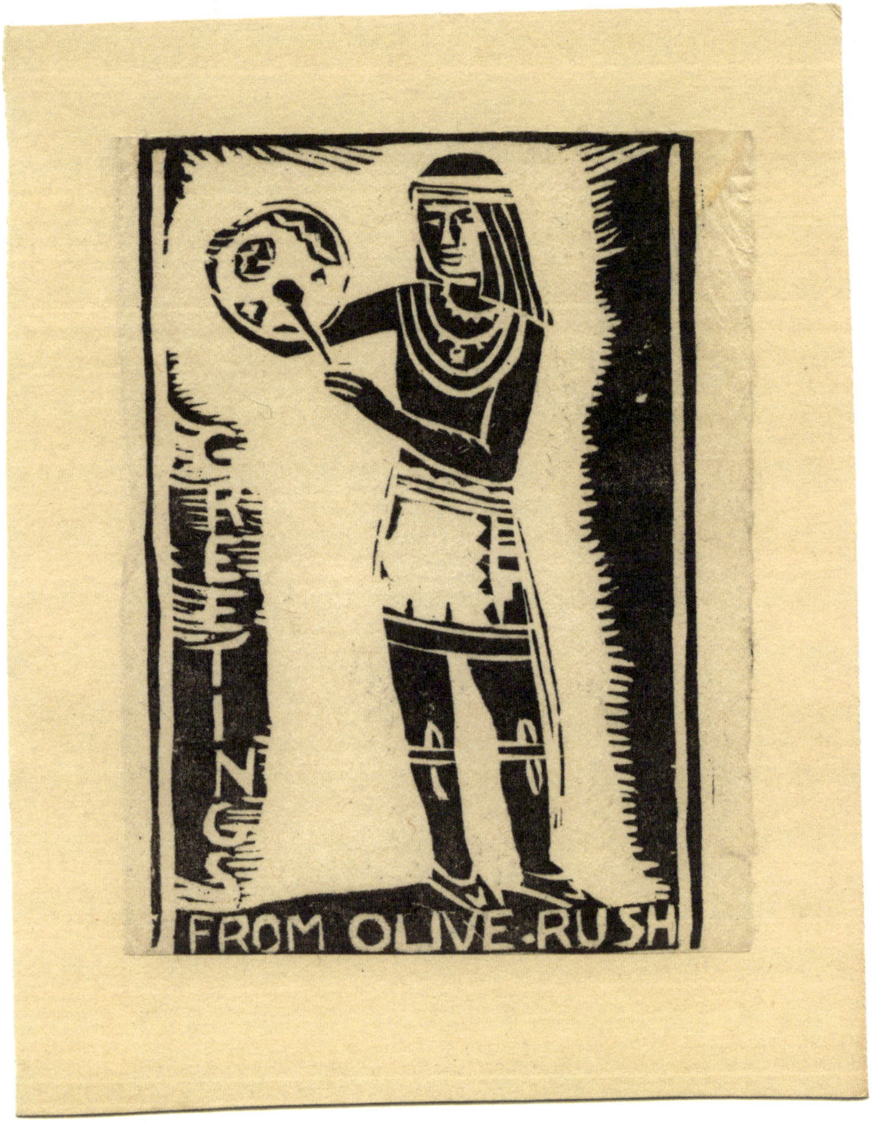

OLIVE RUSH. WOODCUT. UNDATED, CA. EARLY 1930S

Rush, who headed the team that created the murals at the Santa Fe Indian School in 1932, explores native themes with this Indian drummer. Rush met Baumann the day she moved to town in 1920. They remained friends until her death in 1966.

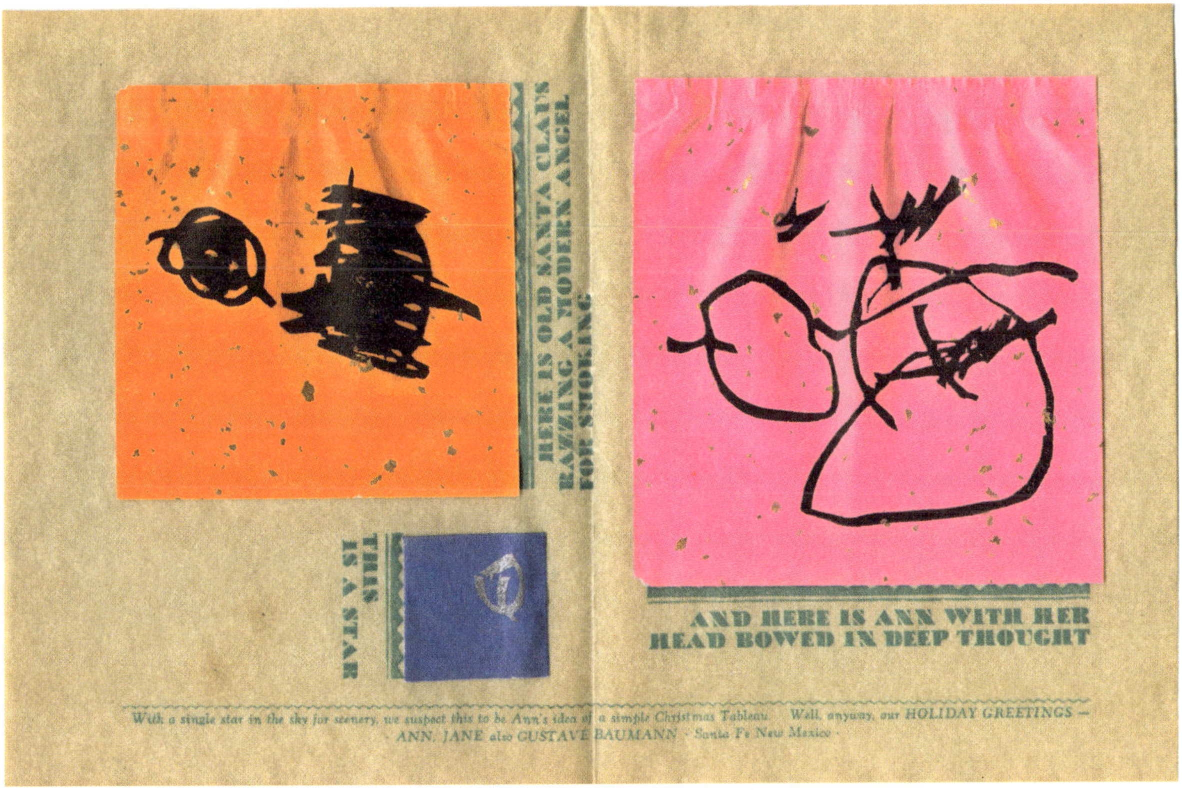

GUSTAVE BAUMANN. WOODCUTS ON COLORED PAPERS. 1931

A father and daughter collaboration, the Baumann's holiday greeting card this year features drawings by four-year-old Ann interpreted as woodcuts by Gus. Samples of the colorful slips of paper still remain in the Press at the Palace of the Governors collection.

HOWARD COOK. WOOD ENGRAVING. 1931

At first glance, the Christmas feast seems to be a scene of domestic tranquility, as if perhaps this is Cook's version of a "Peaceable Kingdom," with cats and dogs sharing a contented holiday meal. But a closer look reveals a more enigmatic scene that might be called "To the Victor Goes the Spoils.

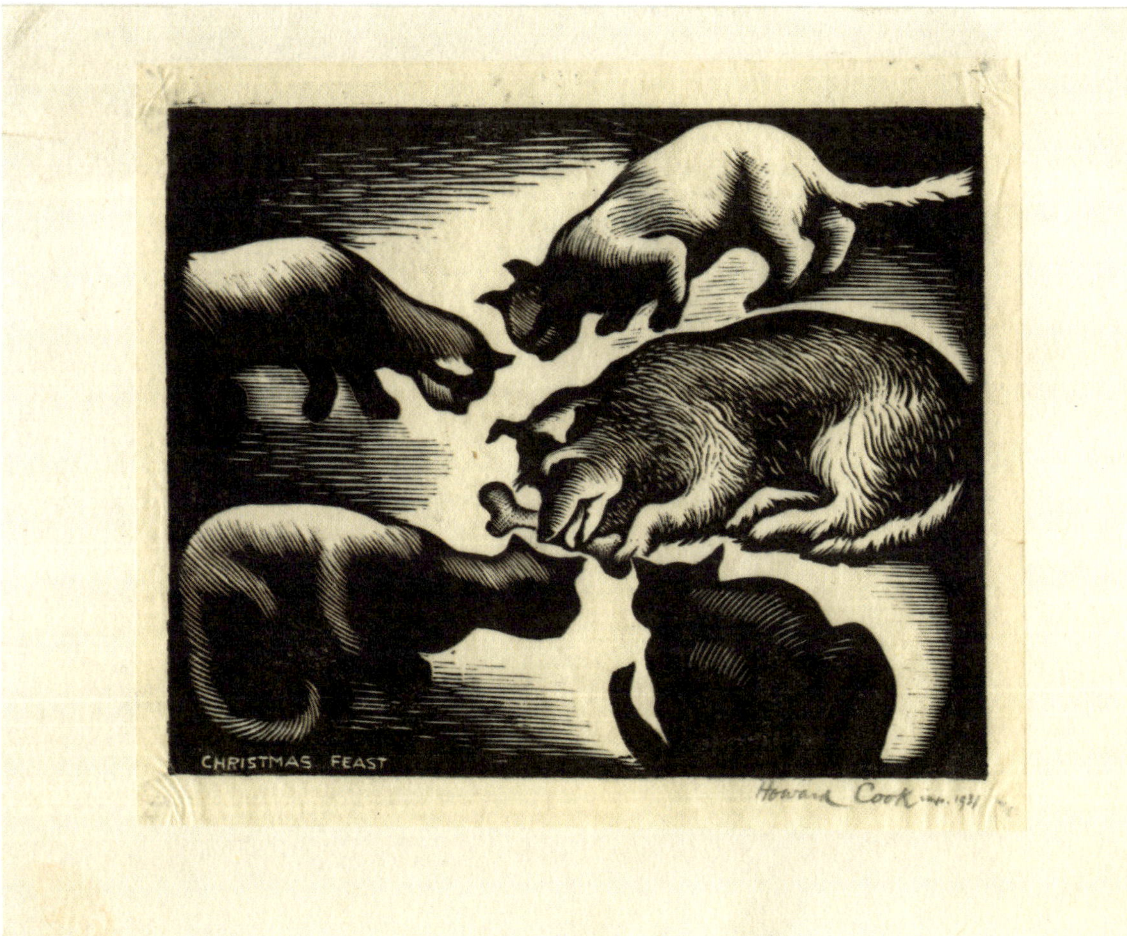

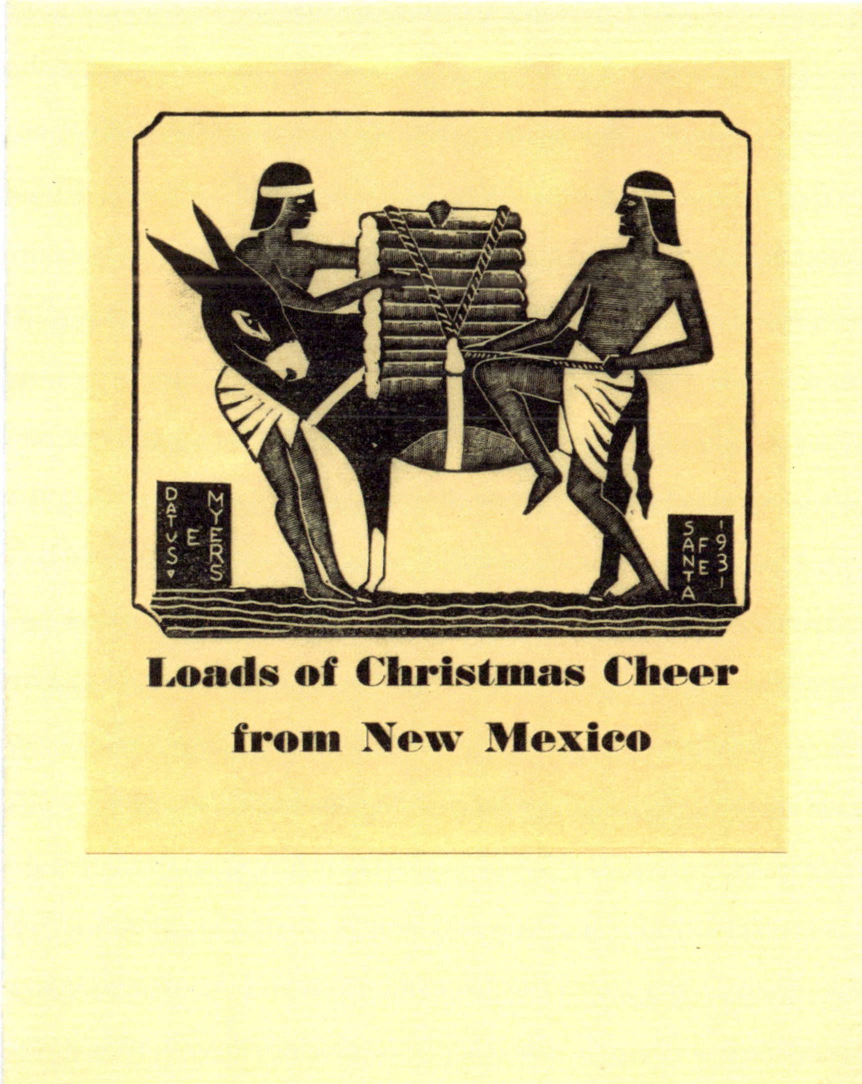

DATUS MYERS. WOOD ENGRAVING. 1931

This highly stylized design reflects the multiple interests of artist Datus Myers. He was the coordinator in charge of Indian artists during the Public Works of Art Project days and was also an avid researcher in Oriental, Egyptian, and American Indian art.

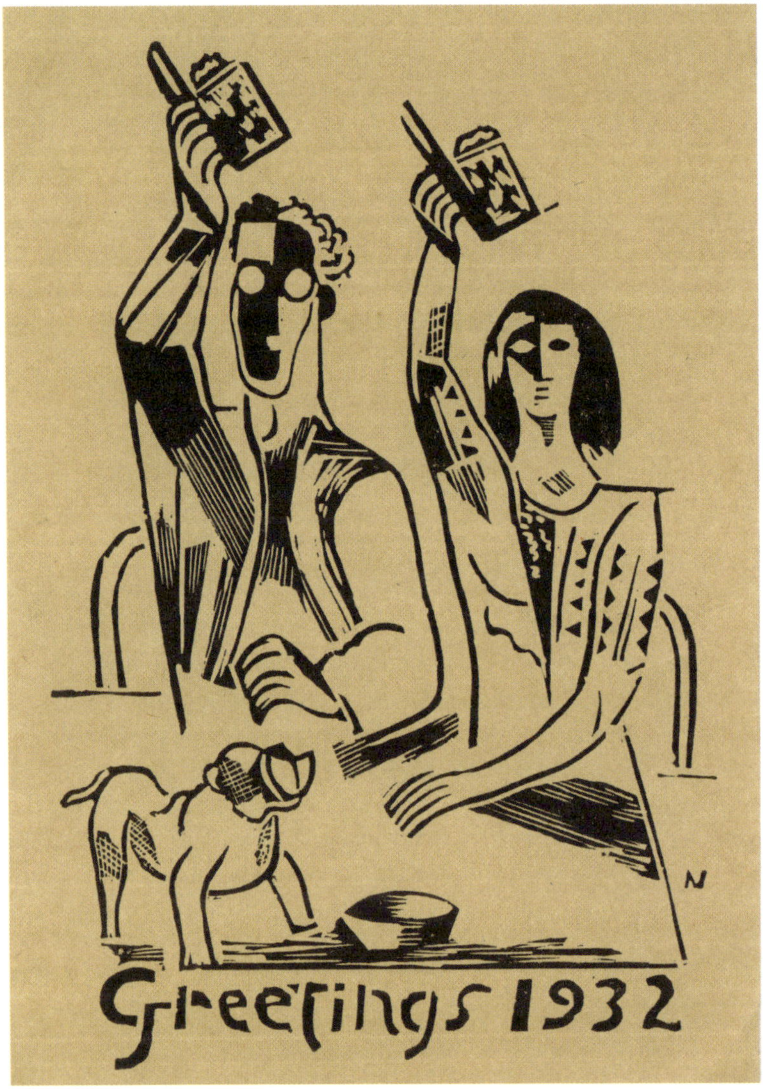

WILLARD NASH. WOODCUT. 1932

Willard and Edith Nash, along with their dog Beau, toast the New Year with mugs of what appears to be beer. Was champagne out of their reach in the depth of the Depression, or were they drinking root beer in this year before the repeal of Prohibition?

PAUL HORGAN. PHOTO-ENGRAVING WITH LETTERPRESS TYPE. 1933

The Pulitzer Prize-winning author Paul Horgan was also a fine artist. Although the Holy Family is a common Christmas card theme, it is rare to see the father of Jesus pictured alone on a holiday card.

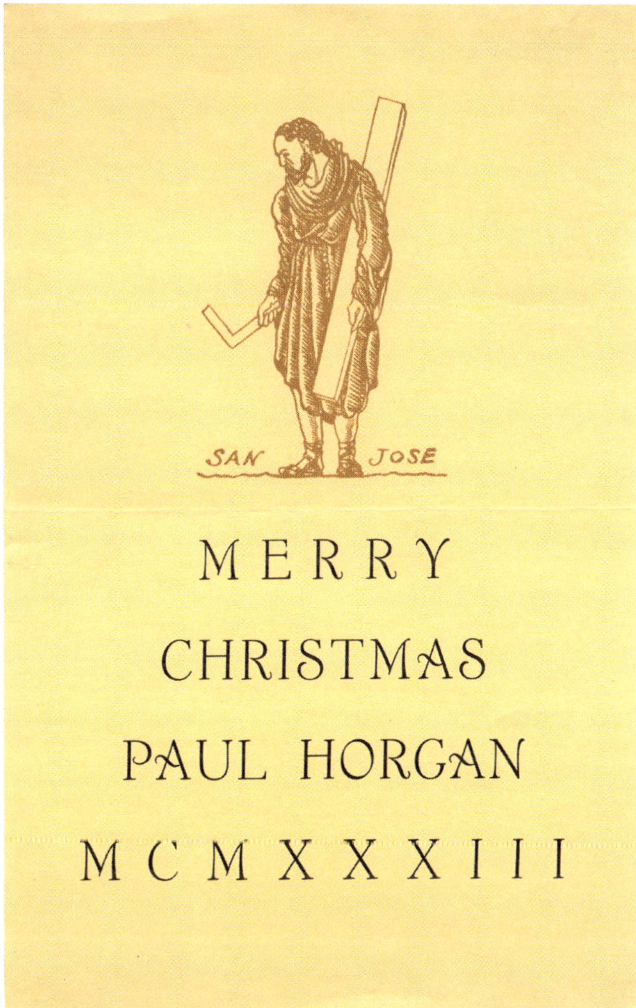

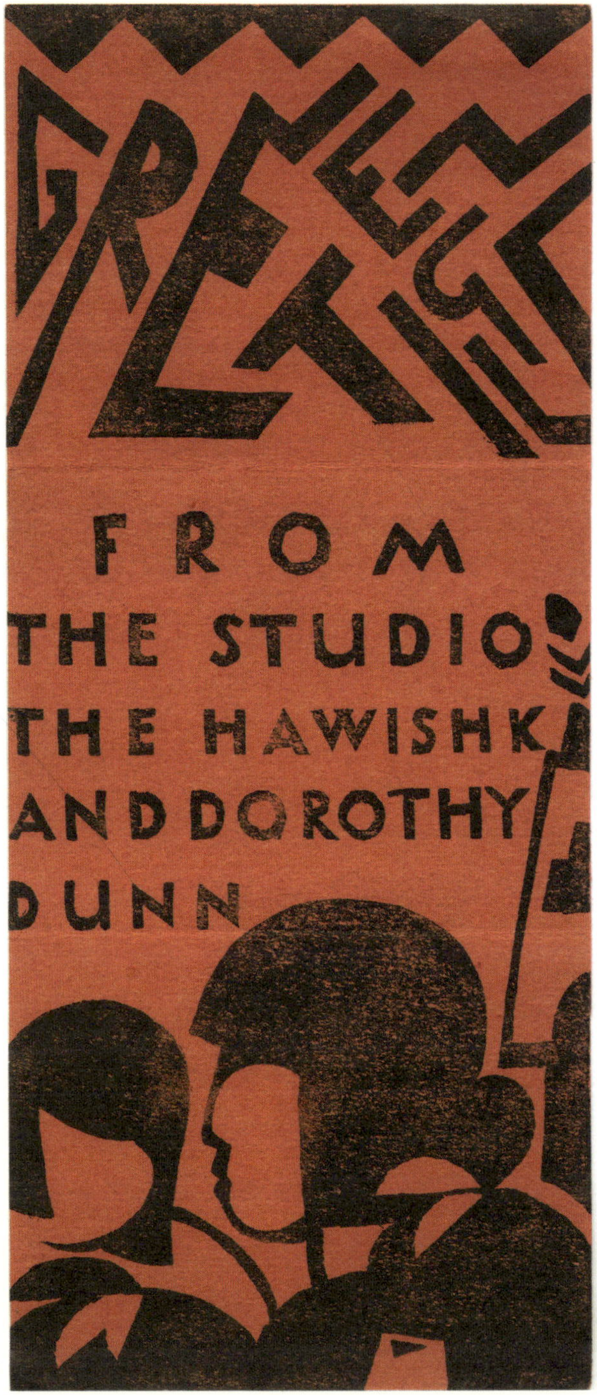

DOROTHY DUNN.
LINOLEUM CUT. 1933

Baumann helped Dunn, whom he had known in Chicago, to establish the art department, which was known as The Studio, at the BIA Indian School in Santa Fe. Who or what "Hawishk" is presents a mystery.

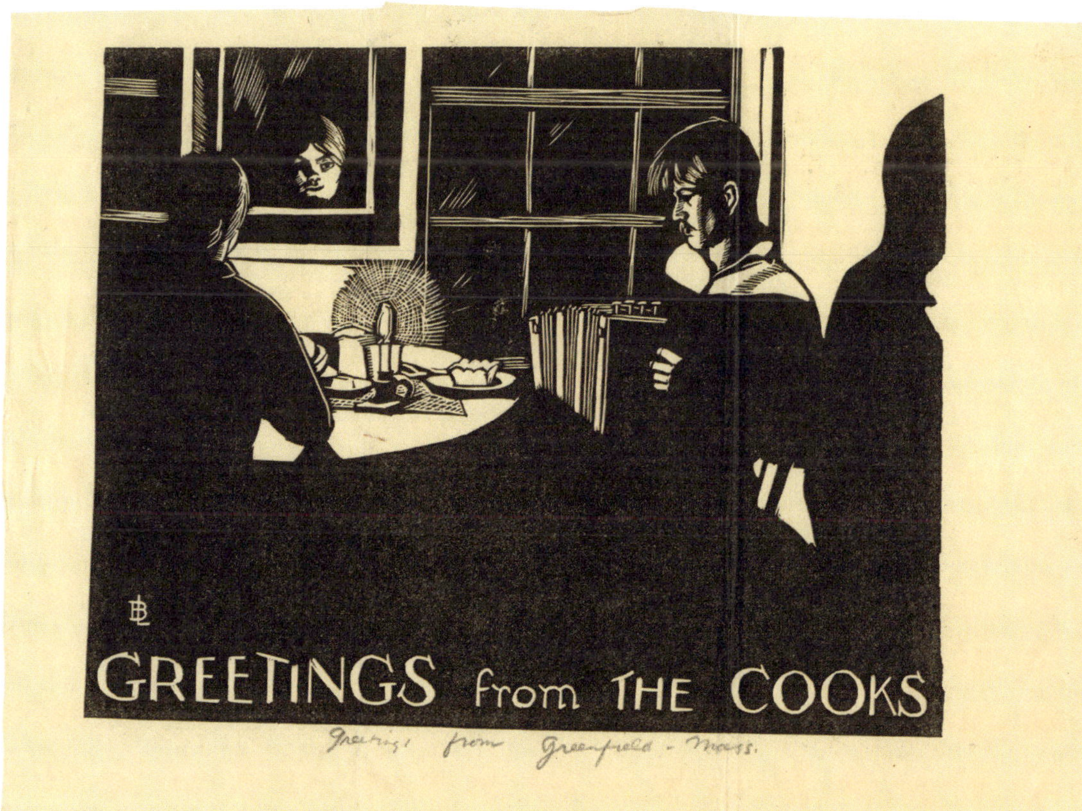

BARBARA LATHAM. WOODCUT. 1933

Taos artists Barbara Latham and Howard Cook are in Massachusetts during the winter of 1933, where Howard is painting murals in the Springfield courthouse. Barbara's self-portrait is reflected in the candlelit window. Perhaps Howard is playing a Christmas carol on the accordion.

GUSTAVE BAUMANN. TWO-COLOR WOODCUT. 1935

The cowboy figure is the concrete sculpture named Billy the Kid modeled by Baumann for the front yard of his house. The poem is characteristically cryptic and typical of Baumann's sense of humor. Although the block for this card was cut by Baumann, it was printed by Willard Clark, who worked with Baumann on a number of projects.

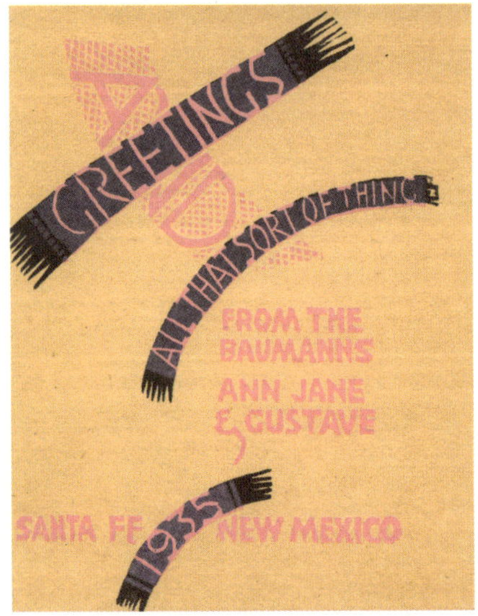

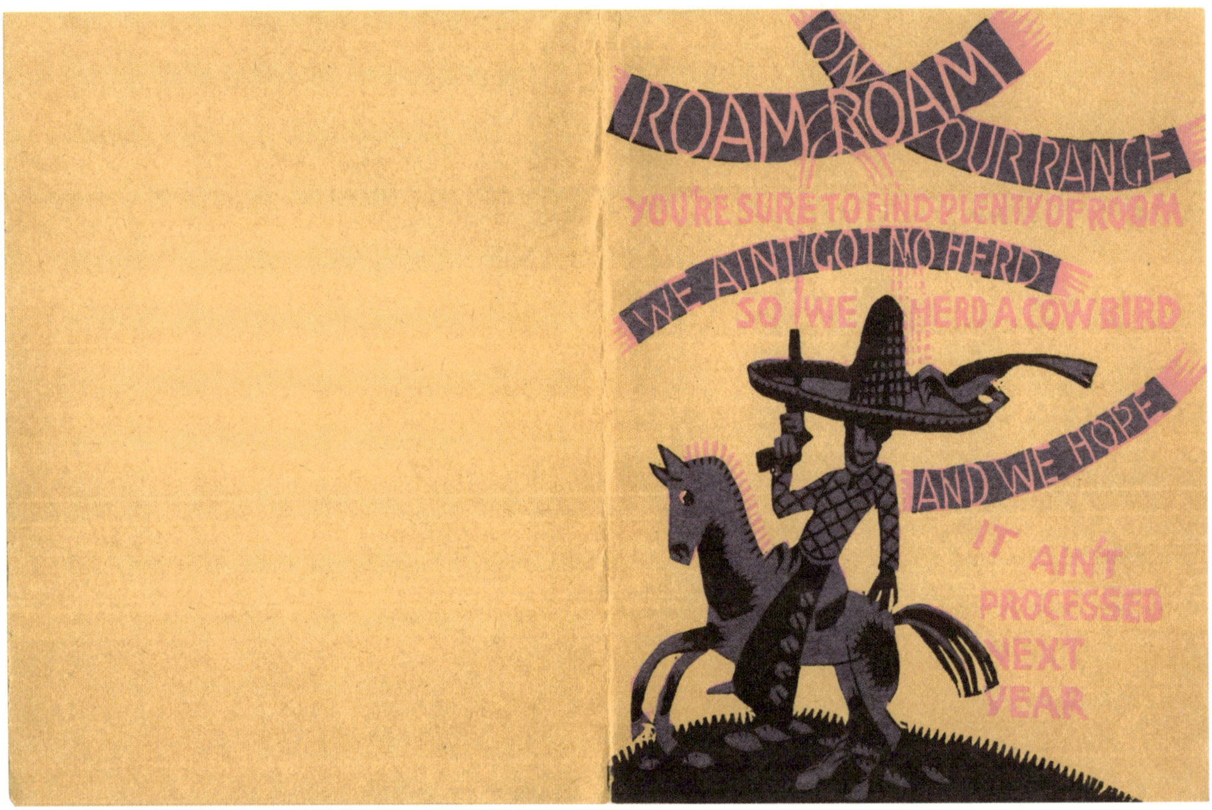

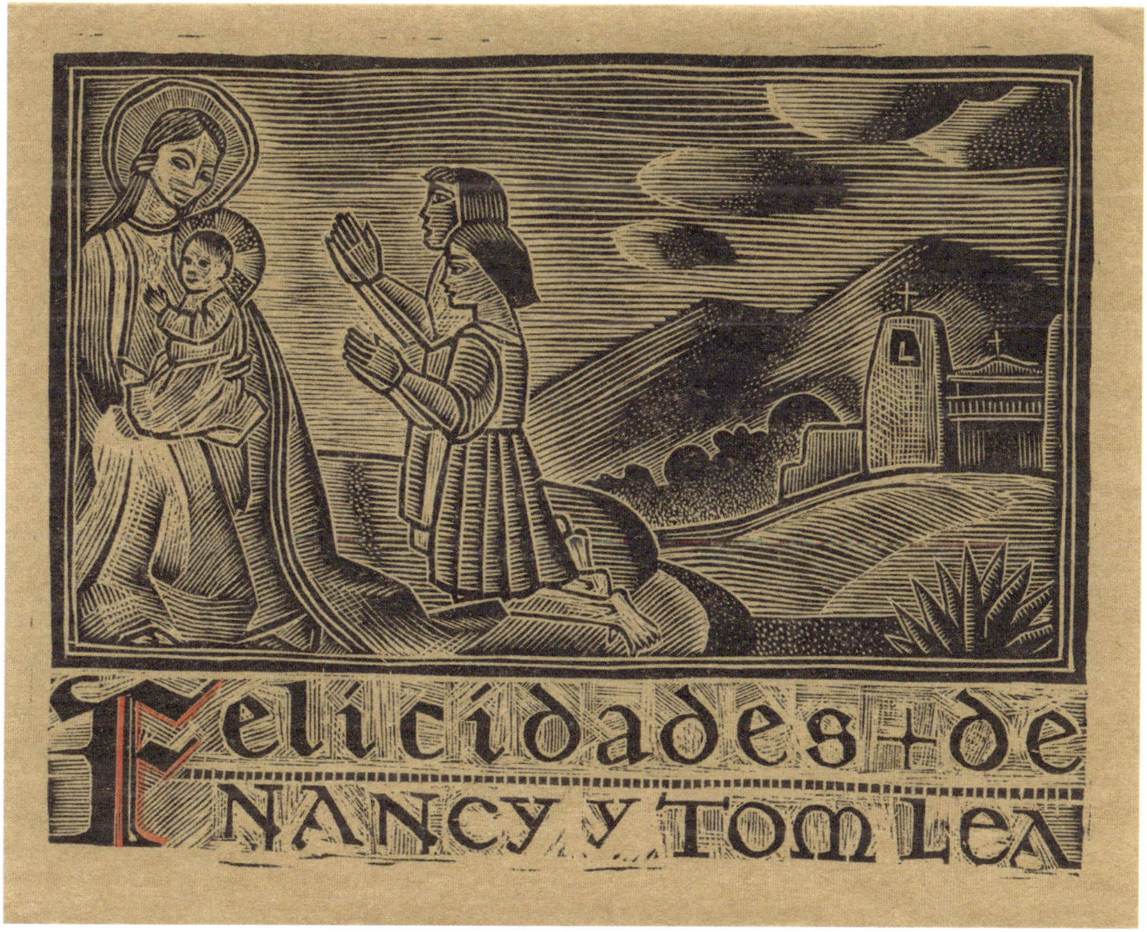

TOM LEA. WOODCUT. 1935

This New Mexican Madonna and Child scene contains echoes of 18th-century Spanish woodcut design. Artist and author Tom Lea and his wife Nancy lived briefly in Santa Fe during the early '30s.

ARTIST UNKNOWN. INK-AND-PENCIL DRAWING ON TORN PAPER BAG. 1930S

Jack and Virginia are unknown to us now, but their humorously poignant Christmas card, which was found in the Baumann archives, sent an obvious message during the Great Depression years.

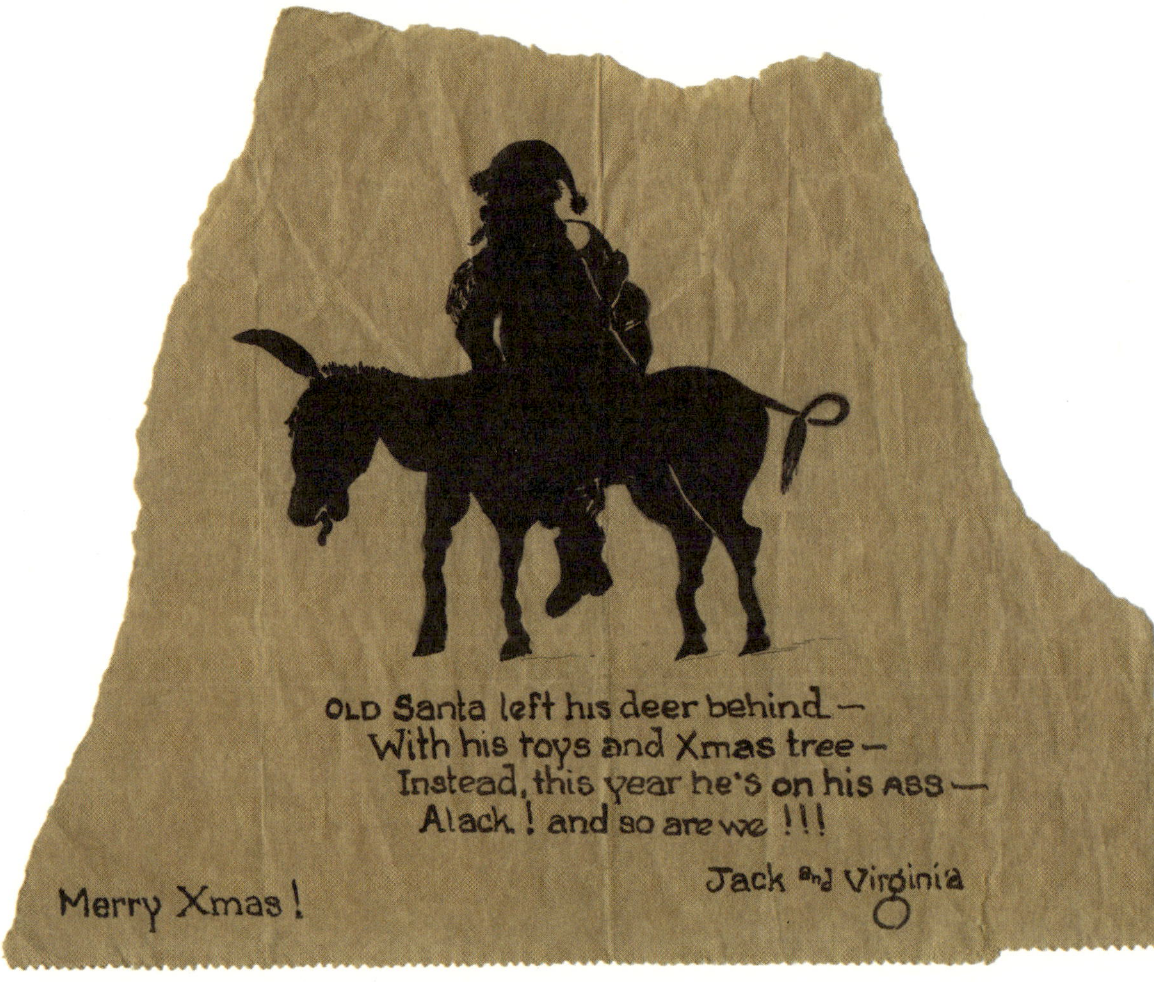

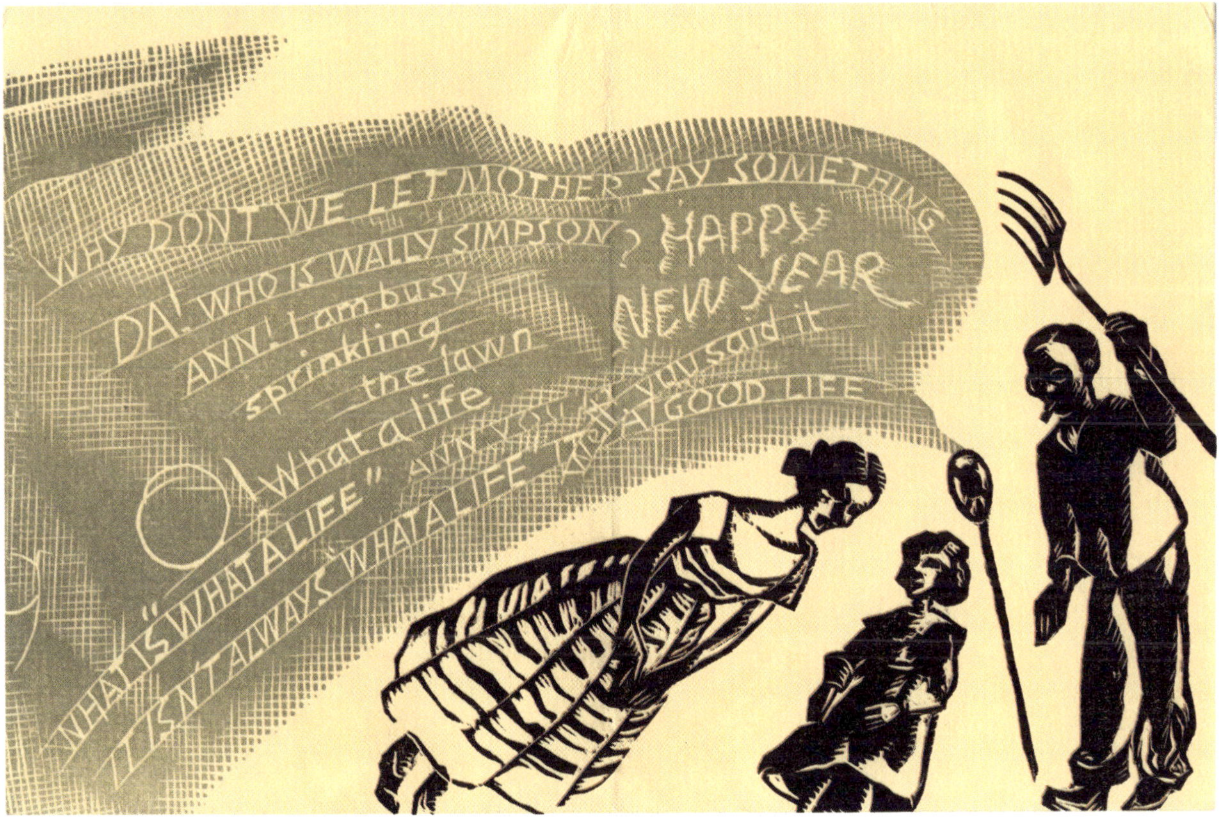

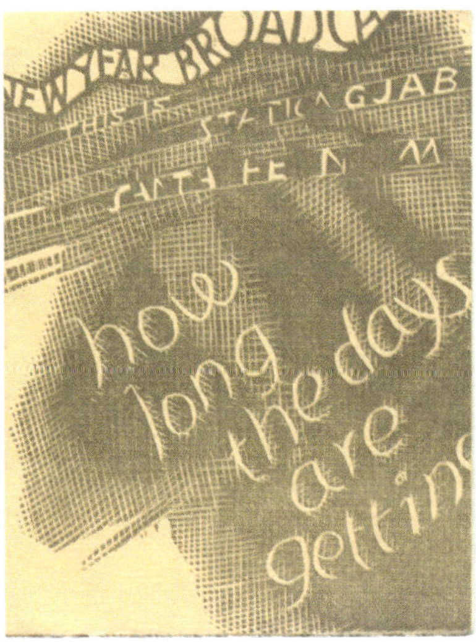

GUSTAVE BAUMANN. TWO-COLOR WOODCUT. 1936

In December 1936, King Edward VIII of England gave up the throne to marry the twice-divorced American Wallis Simpson. International scandal touches even remote Santa Fe.

WILL SHUSTER. PHOTO-ENGRAVING FROM ORIGINAL DRAWING. 1936

Shuster puts on his cartoonist hat for this middle-of-the-Depression greeting sent on a penny postcard.

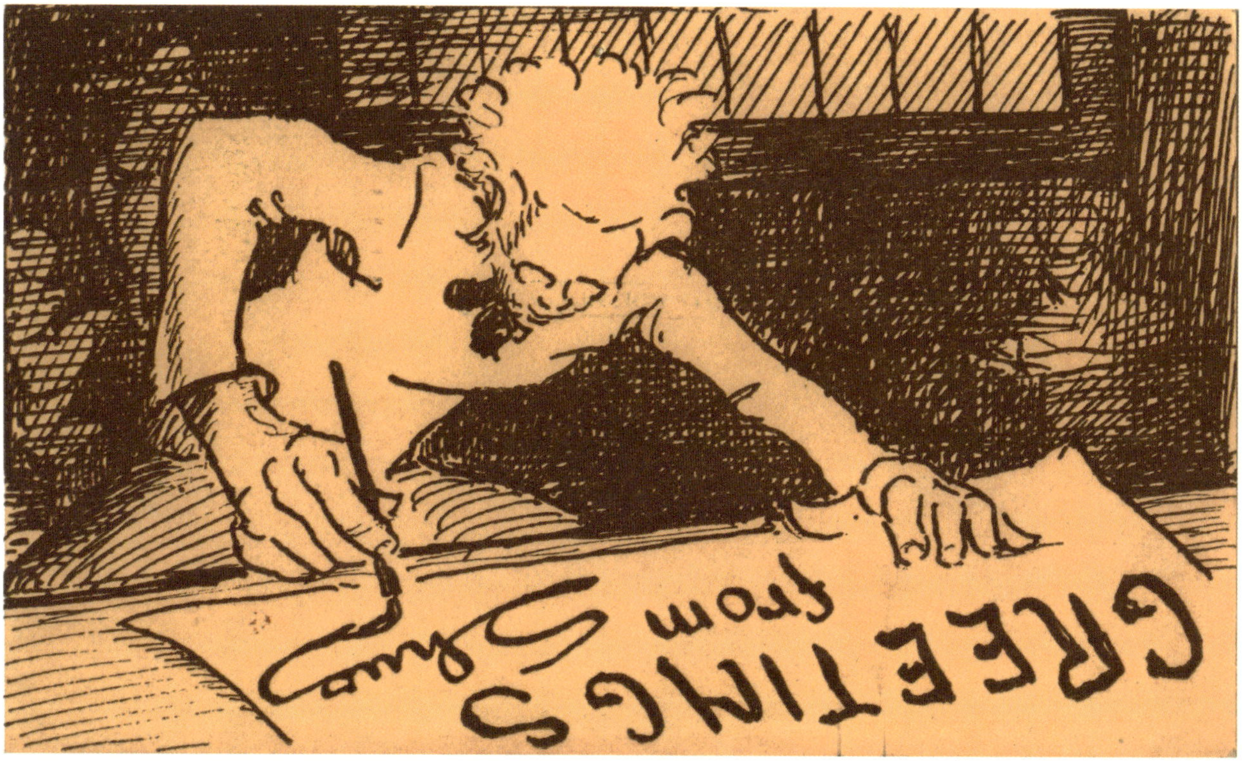

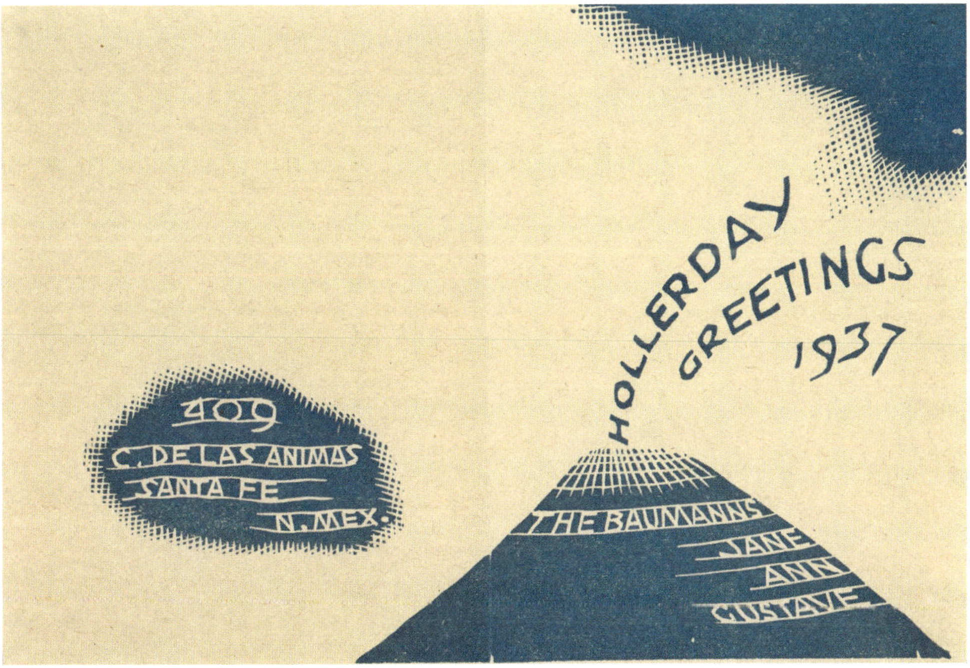

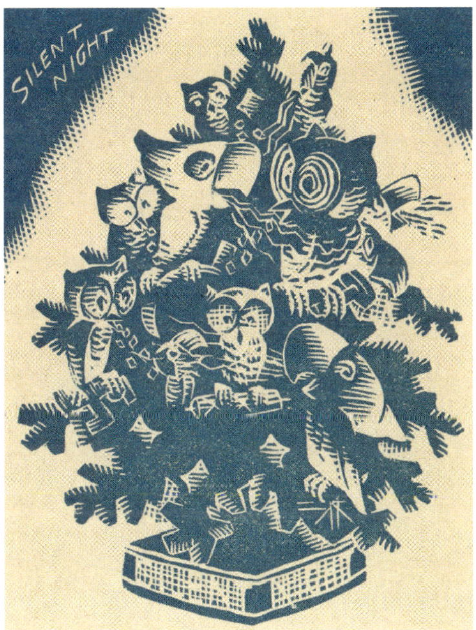

GUSTAVE BAUMANN.
WOODCUT. 1937

Baumann again exhibits his penchant for puns with "Hollerday Greetings" and continues the noise theme inside with a Christmas tree laden with loud birds that he perversely labels "Silent Night."

ERNEST THOMPSON SETON. PHOTO-ENGRAVING FROM ORIGINAL DRAWING. 1938

The naturalist, writer, and artist Ernest Thompson Seton poses with his wife Julia and daughter Dee (Beulah) in a tableau reminiscent of classic depictions of the Holy Family.

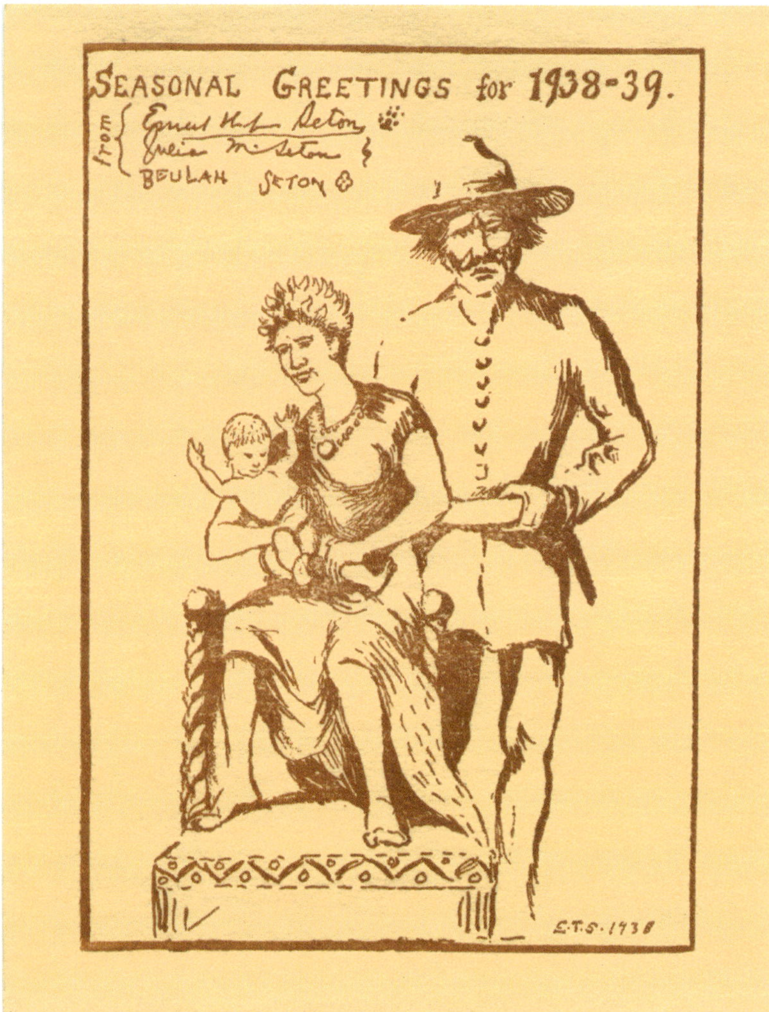

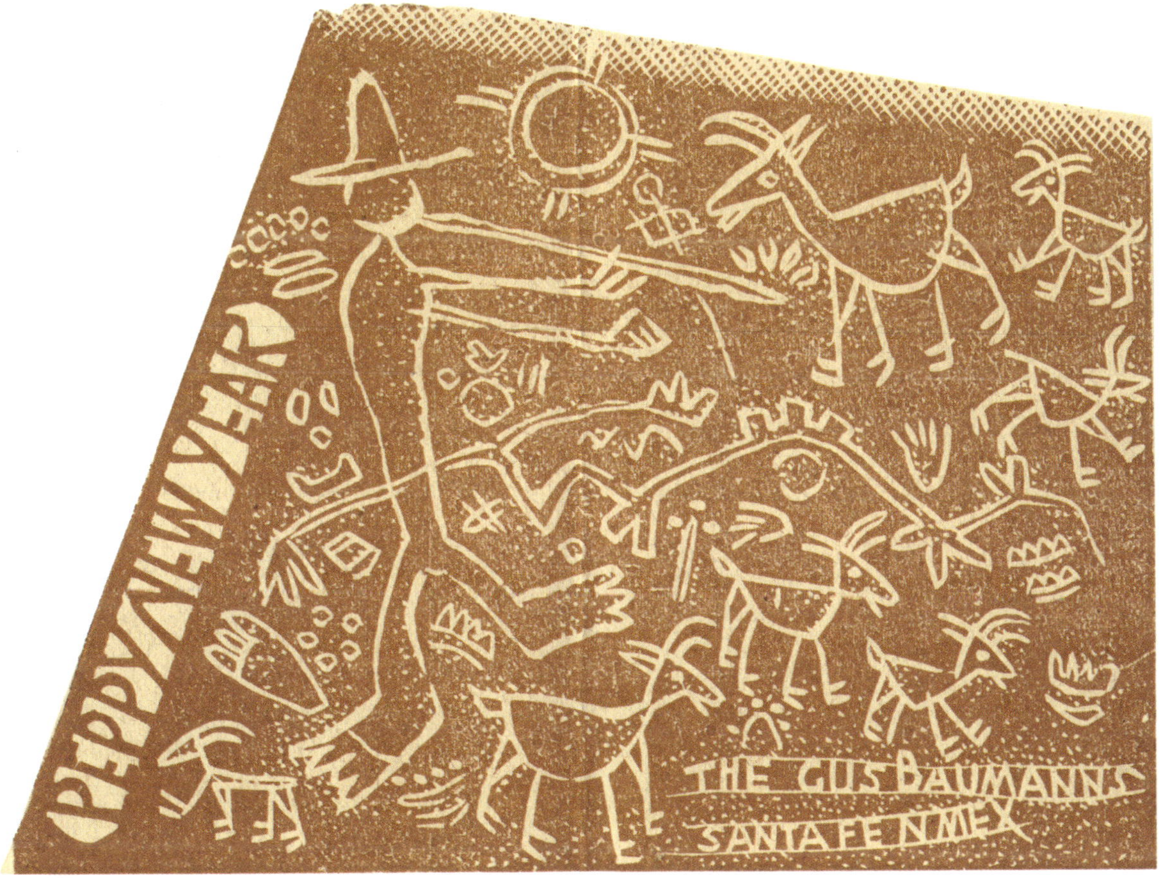

GUSTAVE BAUMANN. WOODCUT. 1939

For this 1939 card, Baumann reconfigures and redesigns images from his book *Frijoles Canyon Pictographs* published that year. The images in the book, with one exception, are accurate drawings of pictographs in Frijoles Canyon in Bandelier National Monument. In that exception Baumann added a hat to an existing figure with the comment, "The ten-gallon hat is my contribution, for certainly a Navaho goatherd able to play a flute obligato to his flock is entitled to wear one."

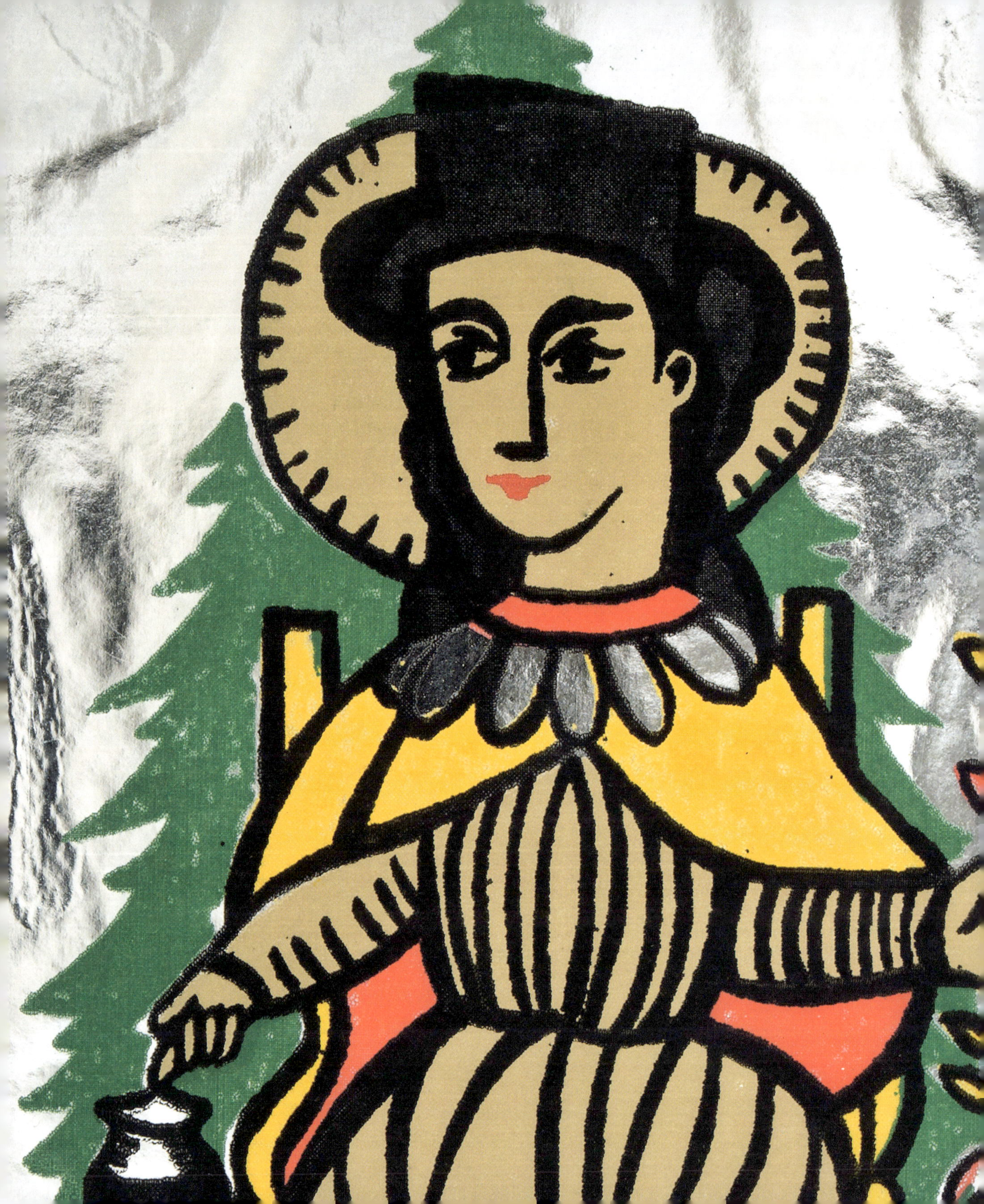

With the Japanese attack on Pearl Harbor in December of 1941, the U.S. was plunged into the largest global war in history. Despite its isolation, New Mexico and its artist colonies were greatly affected. Many families sent members to war or were involved in civil defense or war effort projects. With the end of WWII in 1945, the road back to peace and prosperity engendered optimism and more than a bit of relief.

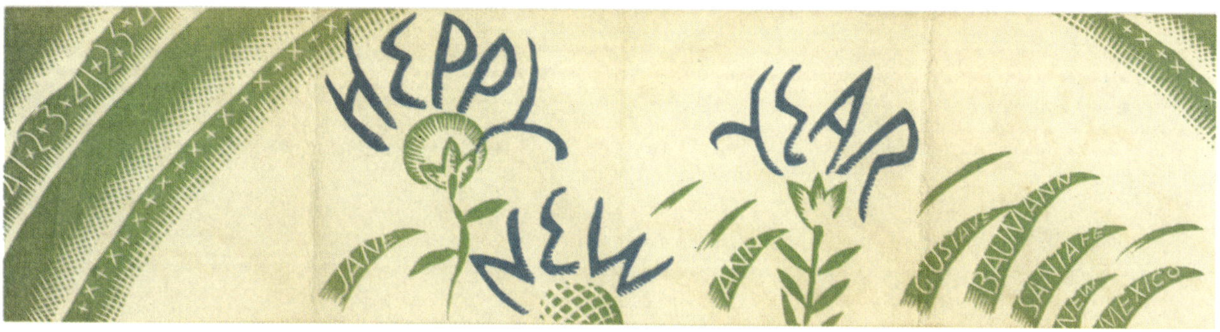

GUSTAVE BAUMANN. TWO-COLOR WOODCUT. 1940

Last year's New Year's card was "Peppy New Year" so of course this year's card must be "Heppy New Year."

WALTER GOODWIN. LETTERPRESS. 1940S

Walter Goodwin, owner and printer of the Rydal Press, uses hand-set type and printers ornaments to compose a charming Christmas card. Goodwin established his publishing operation in Santa Fe in 1933, designing and printing all of the books for the cooperative known as Writers' Editions.

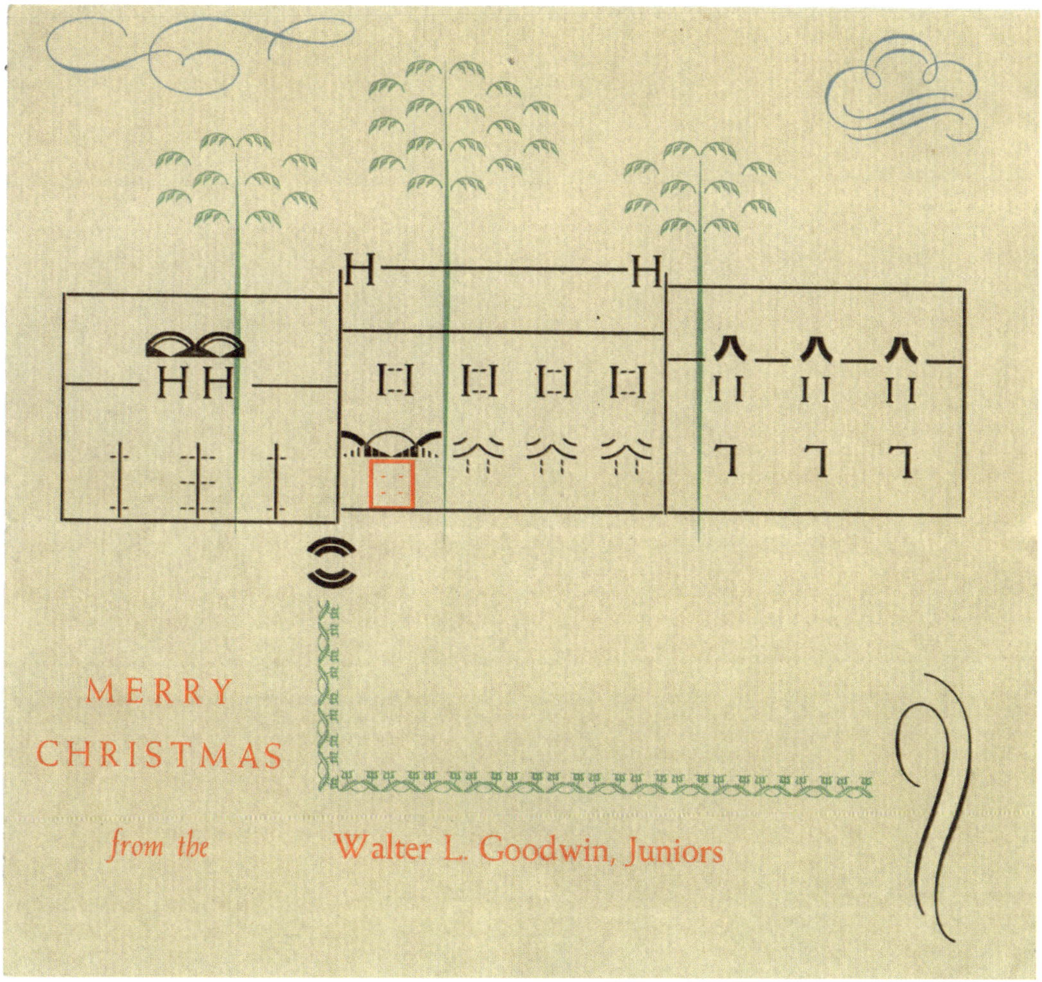

HAROLD E. WEST.
WOODCUT AND
LINOLEUM CUT. 1940

This festive winter party scene is printed from a wood block, while the text is carved from linoleum. West, who was known for his depictions of rural family and cowboy life, met Baumann soon after arriving in Santa Fe. Baumann was a mentor to the younger man in the art of woodcut and gave him some of his first wood blocks.

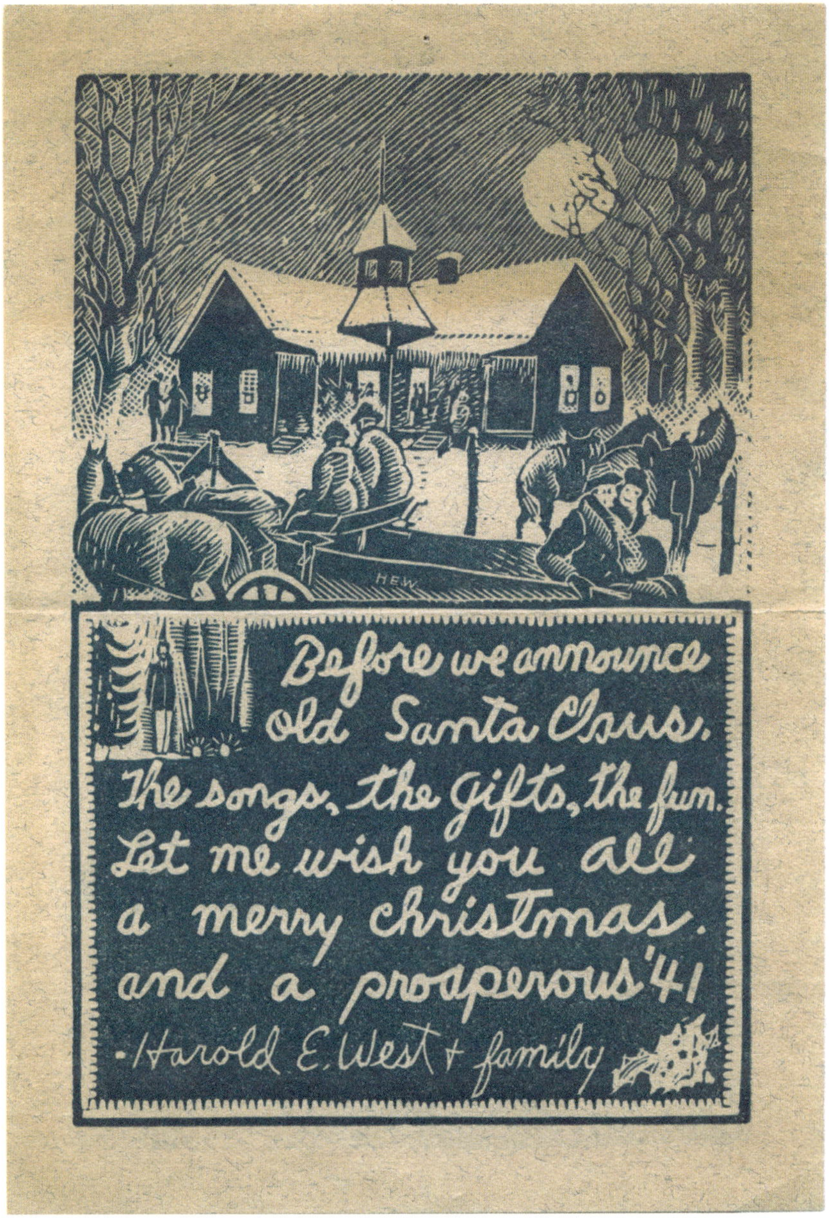

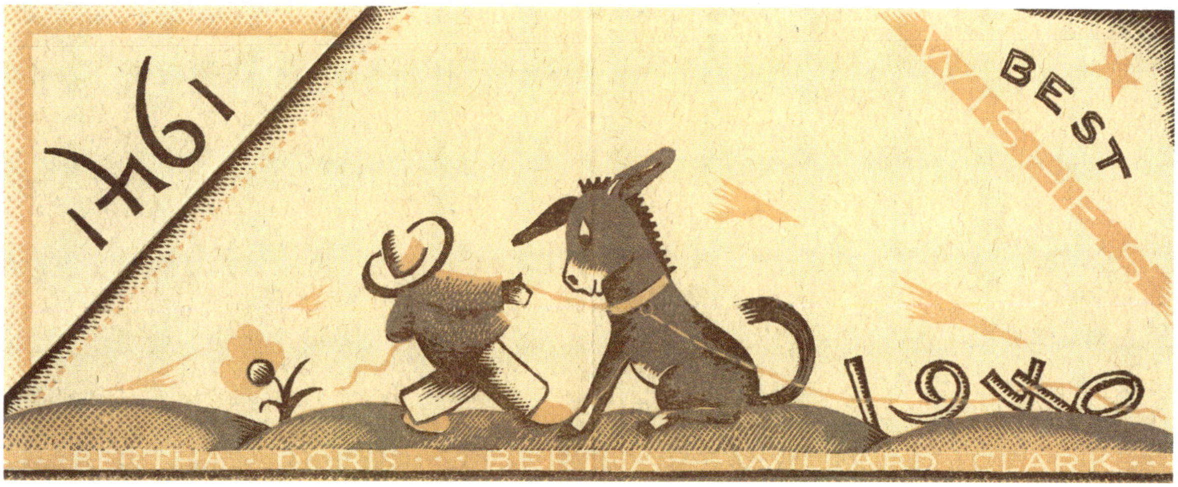

WILLARD CLARK. TWO-COLOR WOODCUT. 1941

The recalcitrant burro who does not want to pull 1940 into 1941 is typical of Clark's humor and imagery. This card was created for himself and his family, but Clark was also a fine printer who produced hundreds of designs for commercial holiday cards in small editions from original wood blocks and hand-set type. Many of the artists and intellectuals of Santa Fe commissioned Clark to make their cards.

OLIVE RUSH. COLOR WOODCUT. UNDATED, CA. 1940S

Using two of the most eloquent symbols for peace, the dove and the olive branch, Rush, a lifelong Quaker, creates a card laden with symbolism and personal reference. She was one of the founders, along with Jane Baumann, of the Santa Fe Quaker Meeting, which meets still in her former house on Canyon Road.

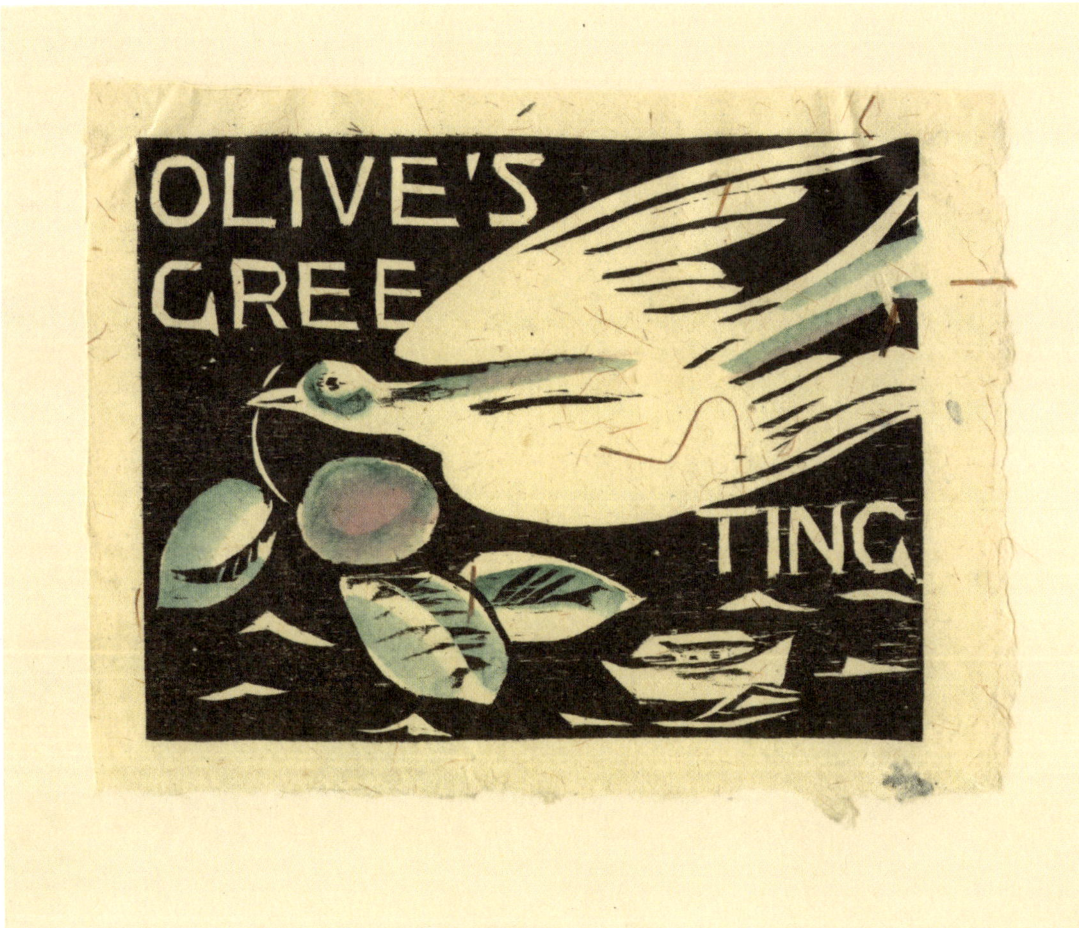

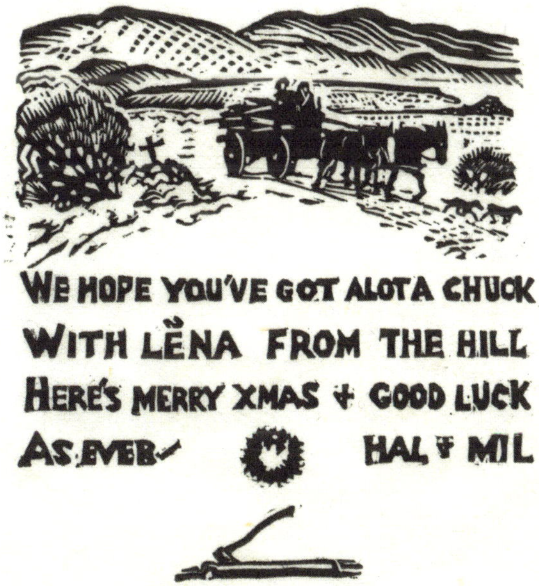

HAROLD E. WEST. WOODCUT. 1941

West creates a typical Northern New Mexico scene with his horse and wagon passing the *descanso* (wayside cross commemorating an accidental death at the site) bringing home firewood from the hills. In *leña*, the Spanish word for firewood, West has misplaced the tilde. In those days in Santa Fe, Spanish was as much the lingua franca as was English. Most of the transplanted artists had large vocabularies in Spanish, but few had the ability to speak or write it with fluency.

GUSTAVE BAUMANN. WOODCUT. 1944

By Christmas 1944, America believed that the war in Europe was nearing an end and that allied forces would probably be victorious. Baumann makes a hopeful forecast showing a rose bud for 1918, the end of WWI, a rose partially opened for 1944, and a fully opened rose with a question mark for the future.

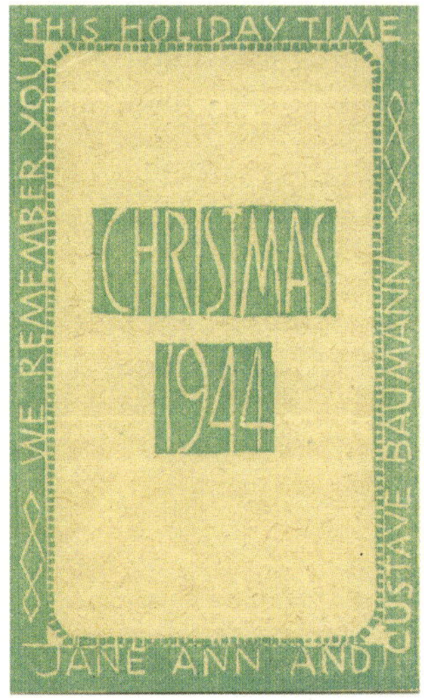

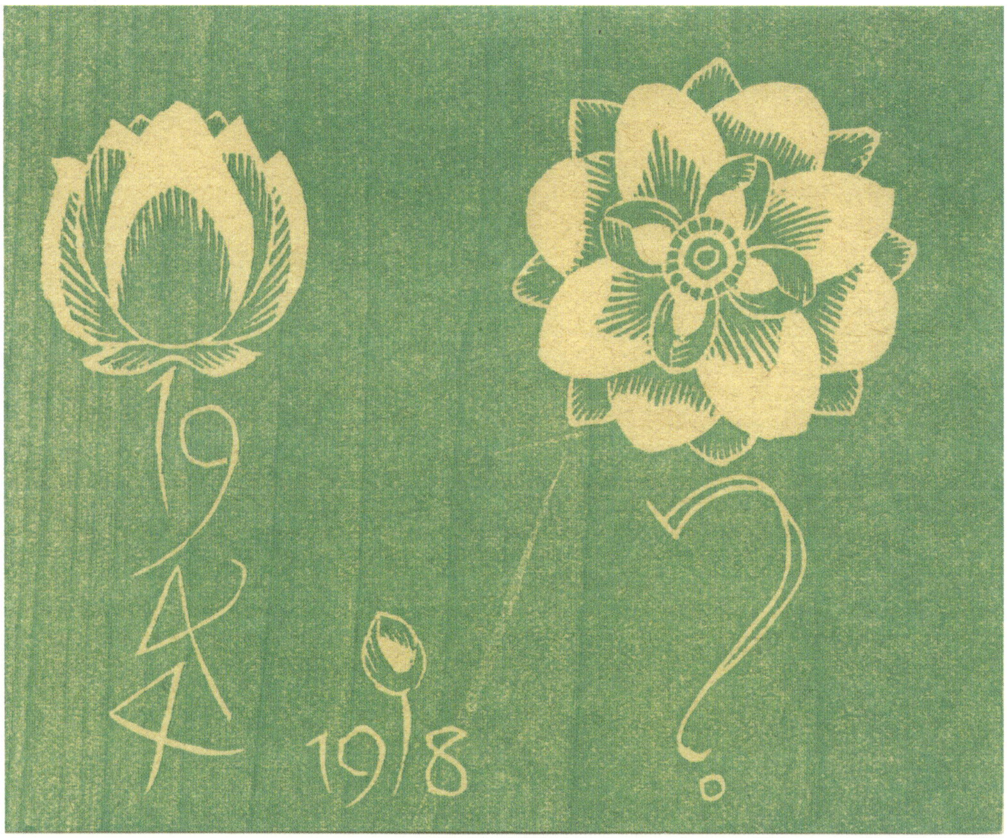

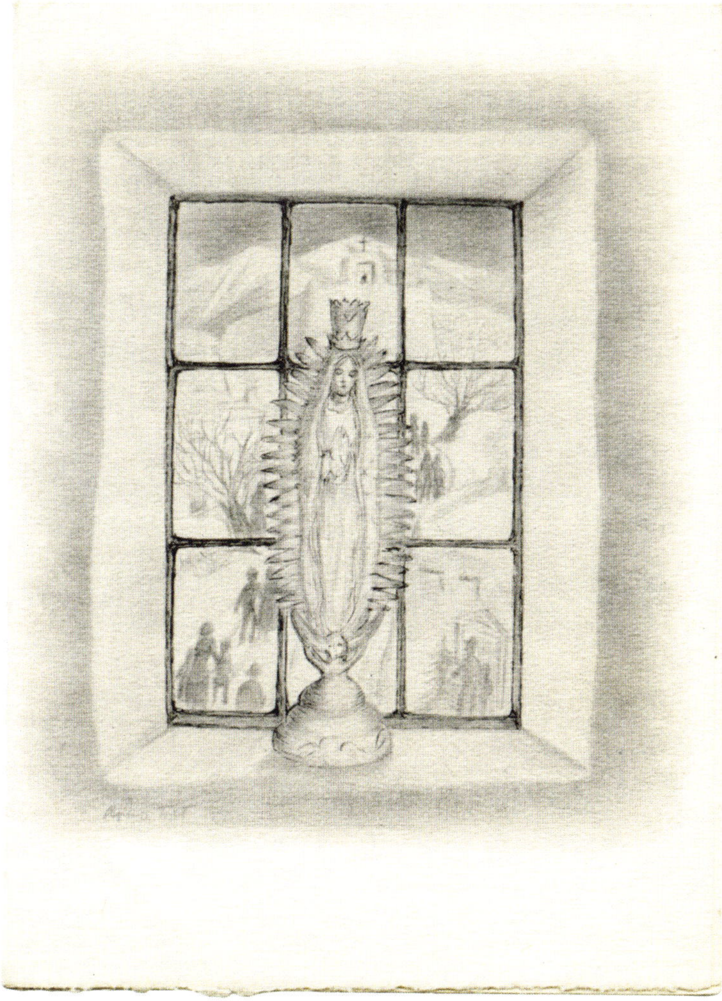

AGNES TAIT. OFFSET LITHOGRAPHY FROM PENCIL DRAWING. UNDATED, CA. 1940S

Tait draws a delicate *bulto* of Our Lady of Guadalupe. The adobe church in the winter scene outside the window surely places this Virgin in northern New Mexico. Tait and her journalist husband, William McNulty, moved to Santa Fe in 1941, where she lived for the next forty years.

JOSEPH IMHOF.
LITHOGRAPH. 1940S

Taos painter and lithographer Imhof uses a Koshare figure for this holiday card. When the Koshare appear at Pueblo religious festivals they not only entertain the crowd with their antics and tricks but serve as social mediators. Their outrageous behavior, which often inverts the mores of the community, works as a warning to those who would transgress. This Koshare, in typical fashion, has inverted the "Season's Greetings."

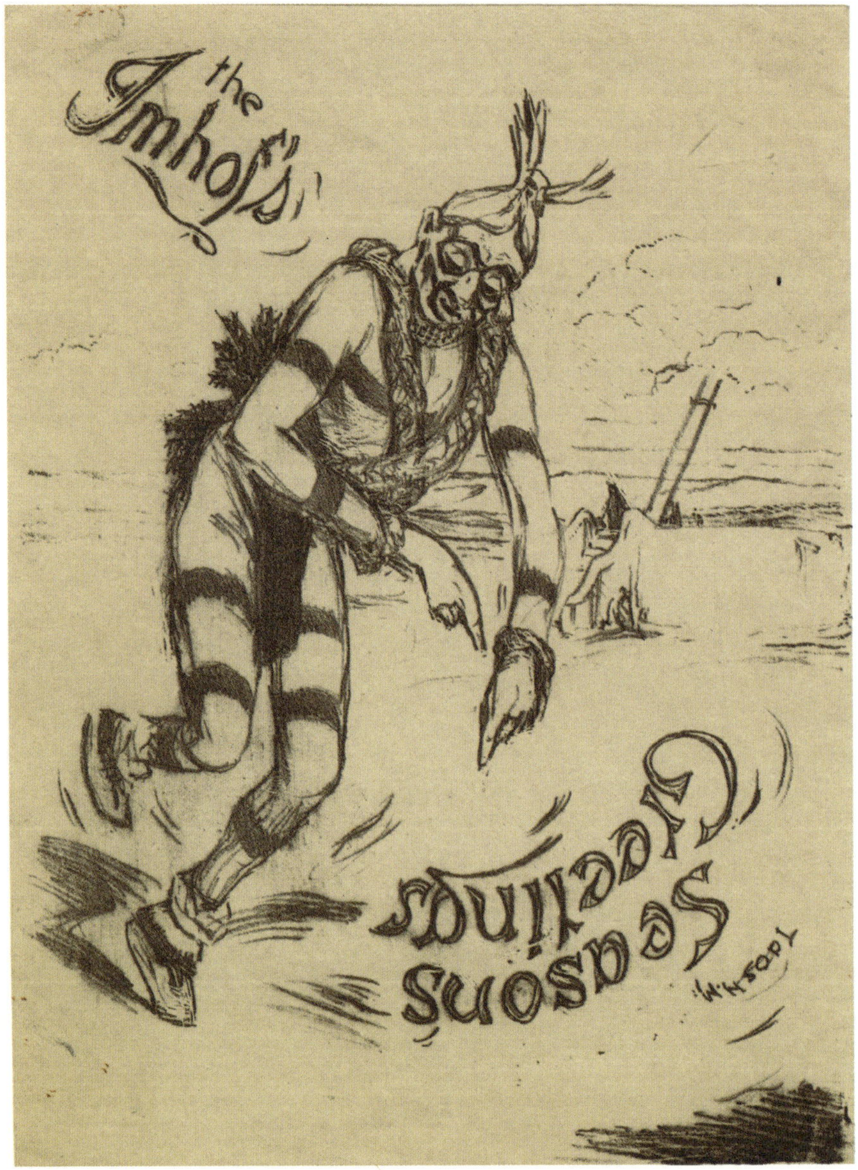

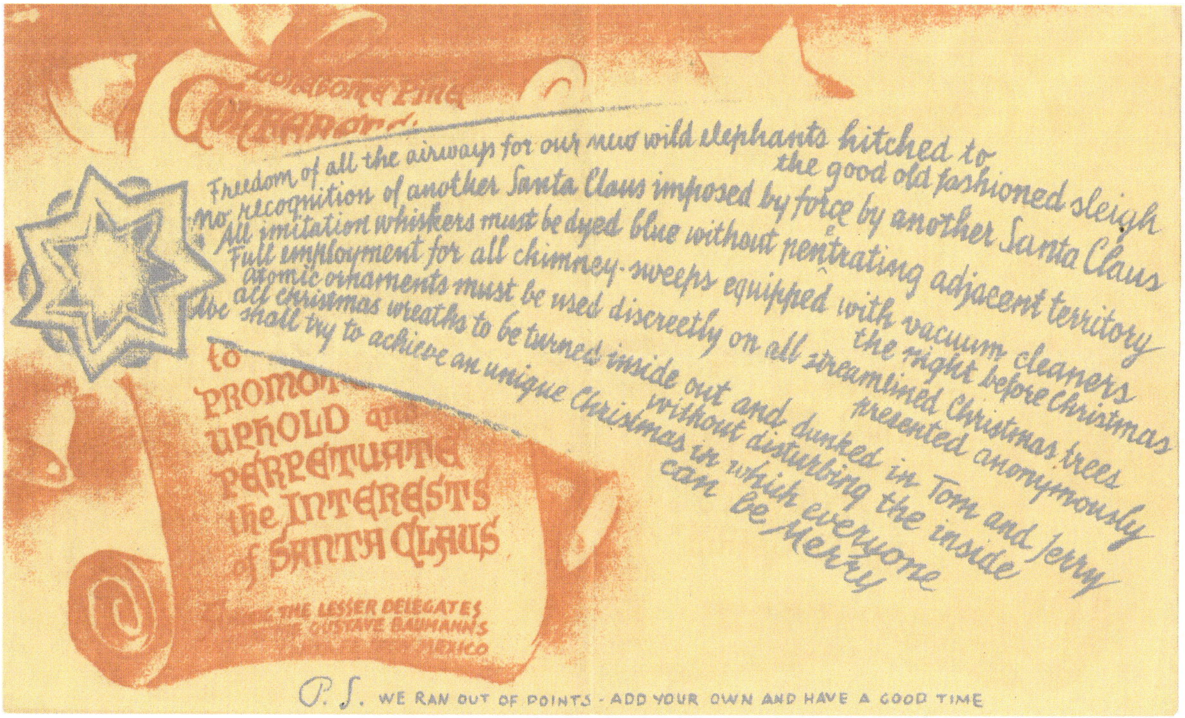

GUSTAVE BAUMANN. SERIGRAPH. 1945

Christmas 1945. The war has been over for almost five months. We can get back to frivolous things, like perpetuating the interests of Santa Claus on a panoramic fold-out card. Silkscreen was a little-used technique in Baumann's repertoire, so it is unknown if he printed this design.

JOHN GAW MEEM. DIAZOPRINT. UNDATED, CA. 1940S

Santa Fe architect John Gaw Meem, best known for his influence in the development of the Pueblo Revival Style, uses architectural paper and the blue line process for his family Christmas card. Every Christmas in the Meem house, these *bultos* of the Holy Family were brought out and placed on the little *repisa* (shelf) in the front hallway.

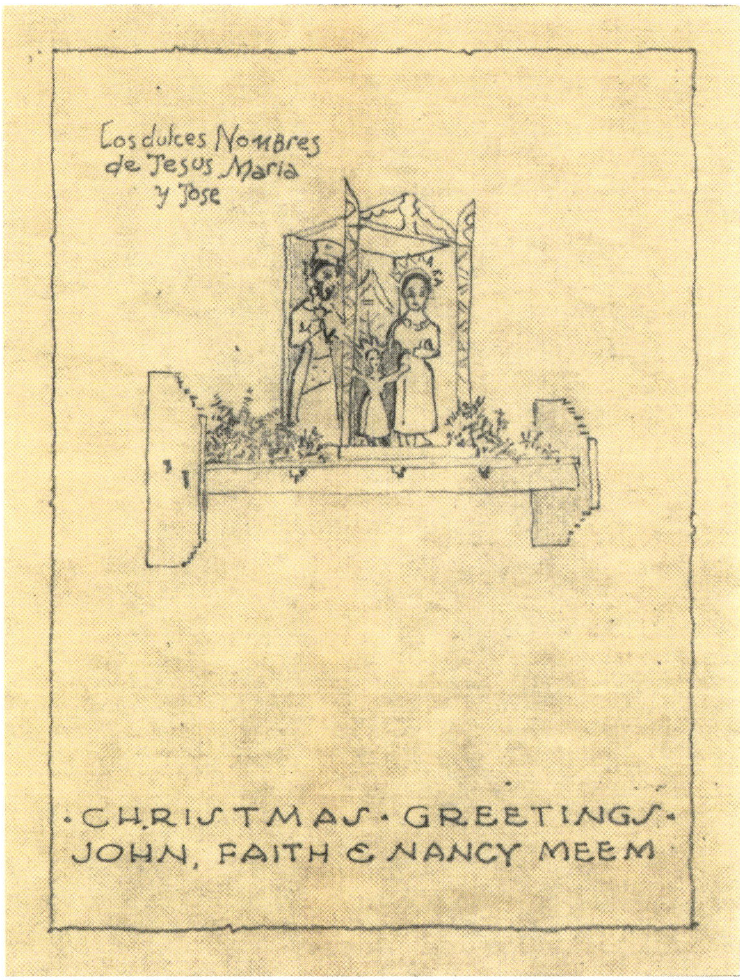

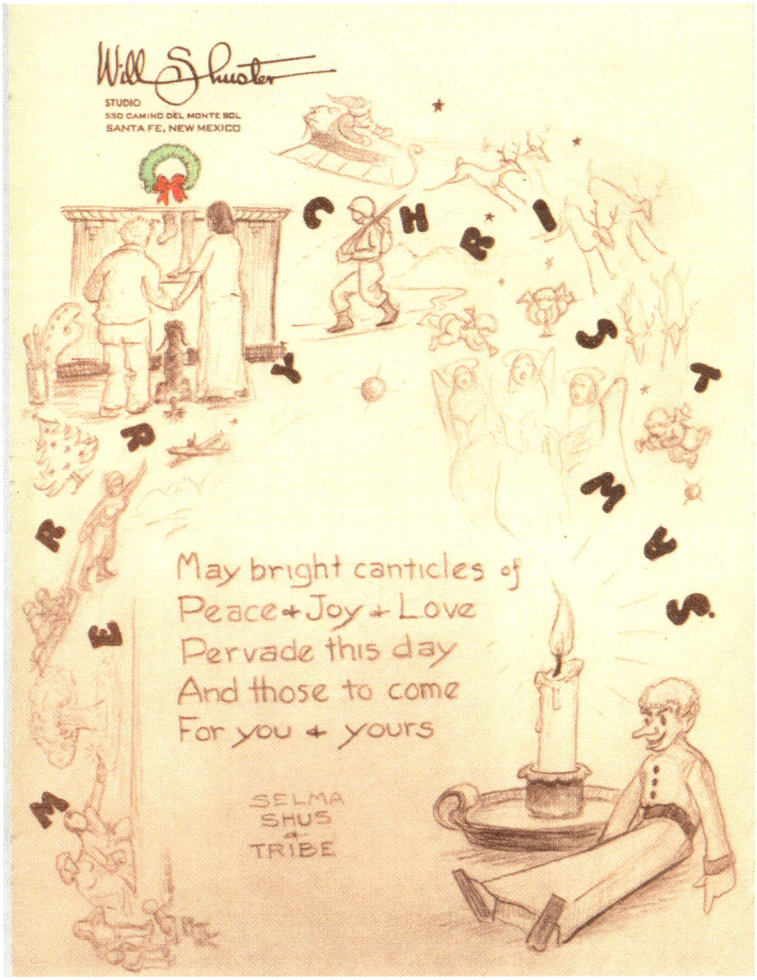

WILL SHUSTER. OFFSET LITHOGRAPHY FROM ORIGINAL DRAWING. 1945

The war is over. A joyous time for most Americans, the end of WWII would have had great significance for Shuster, whose own experiences in the First World War had left him partially disabled. His son, Don, fought in the European theater but survived and made it home to Santa Fe just in time for Fiesta. This wonderful card appears to be a page of doodles, but when carefully examined it reveals drawings of disparate emotion: The painter and his wife in front of the Christmas hearth, family fun in the snow, an atomic mushroom cloud, a grinning Zozobra next to a burning candle, a returning soldier, and Santa Claus with a host of singing angels.

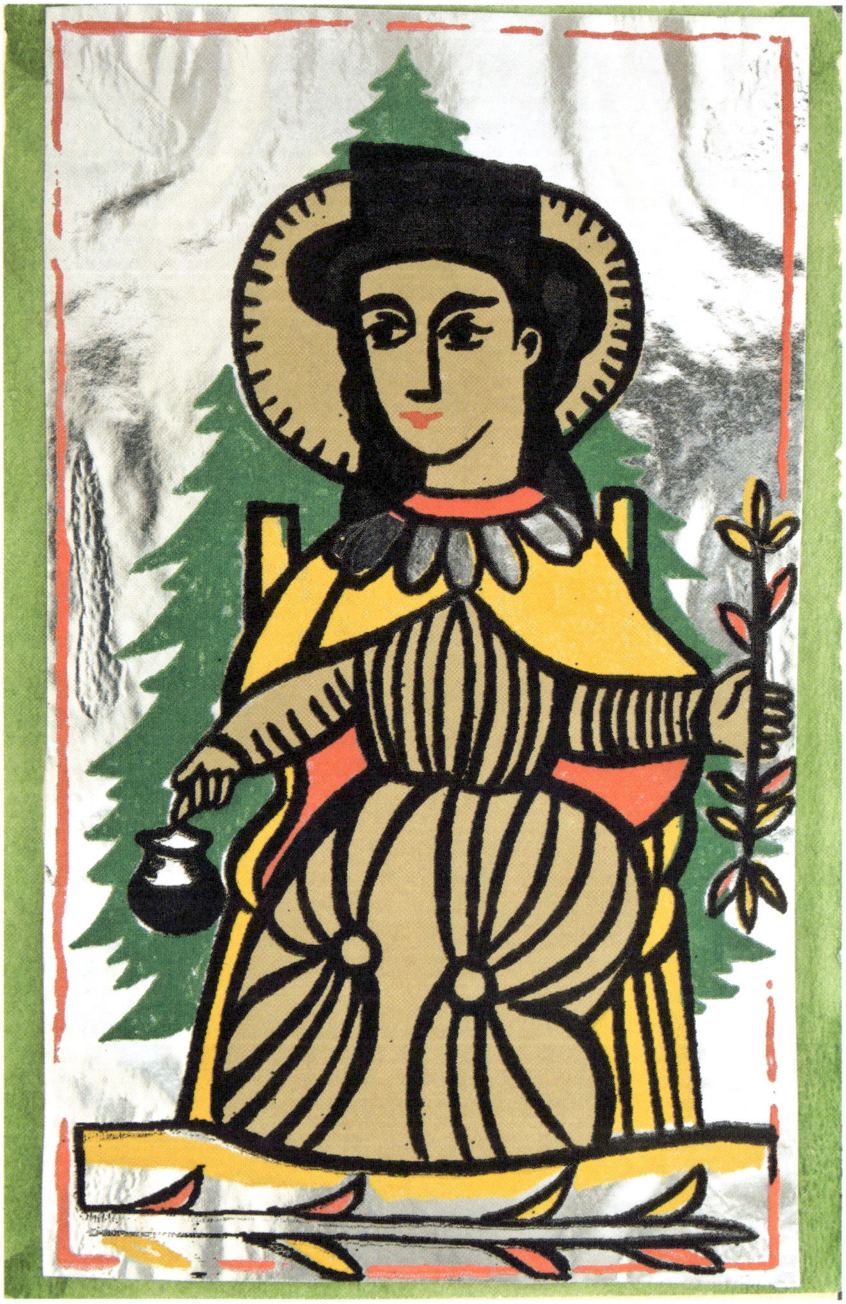

LOUIE EWING. SERIGRAPH ON SILVER FOIL PAPER. UNDATED, CA. 1940S–1950S.

Louie Ewing, who was a master of the silk screen process, uses an image of Santa Niño de Atocha in front of a Christmas tree as a Christmas card.

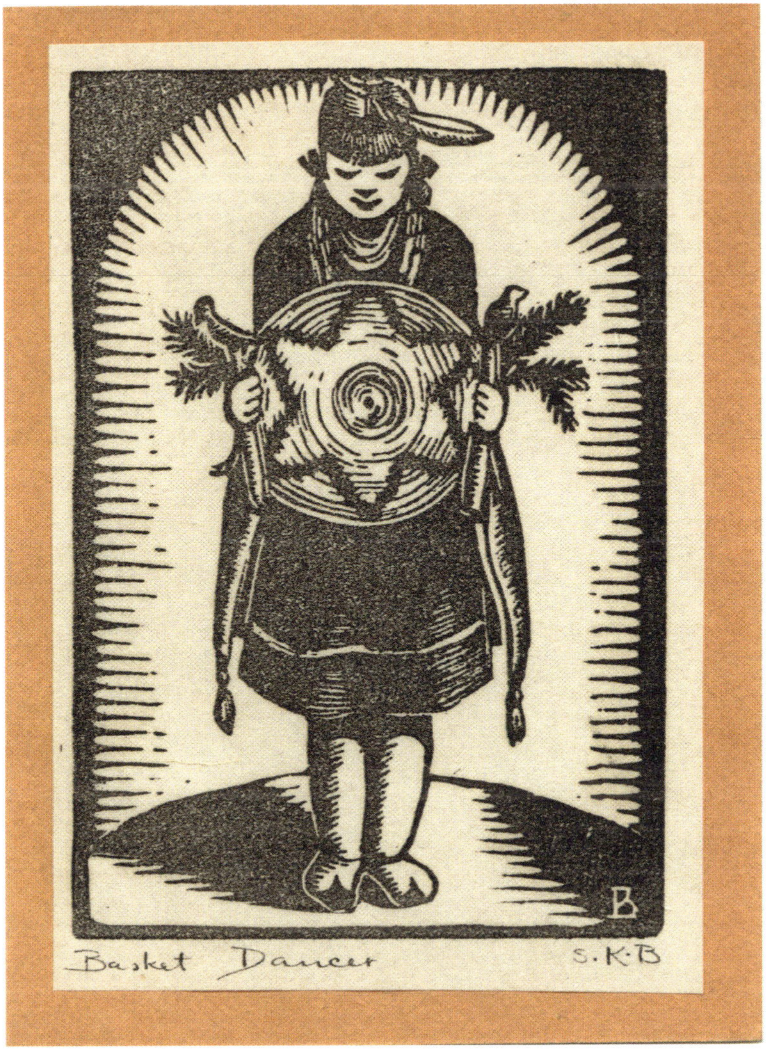

SUZANNE KUTKA BOSS. WOODCUT. 1947

Suzanne and her husband, Homer Boss, for many years spent summers at San Juan Pueblo, where they had many friends and were given Indian names. Both Suzanne and Homer painted portraits of their Pueblo friends, and this design may be based on one of those paintings.

GUSTAVE BAUMANN. WOODCUT. 1948

Hope for the world in the New Year: The European Recovery Program, known as the Marshall Plan, was developed in 1947 to provide economic support to rebuild the European economies.

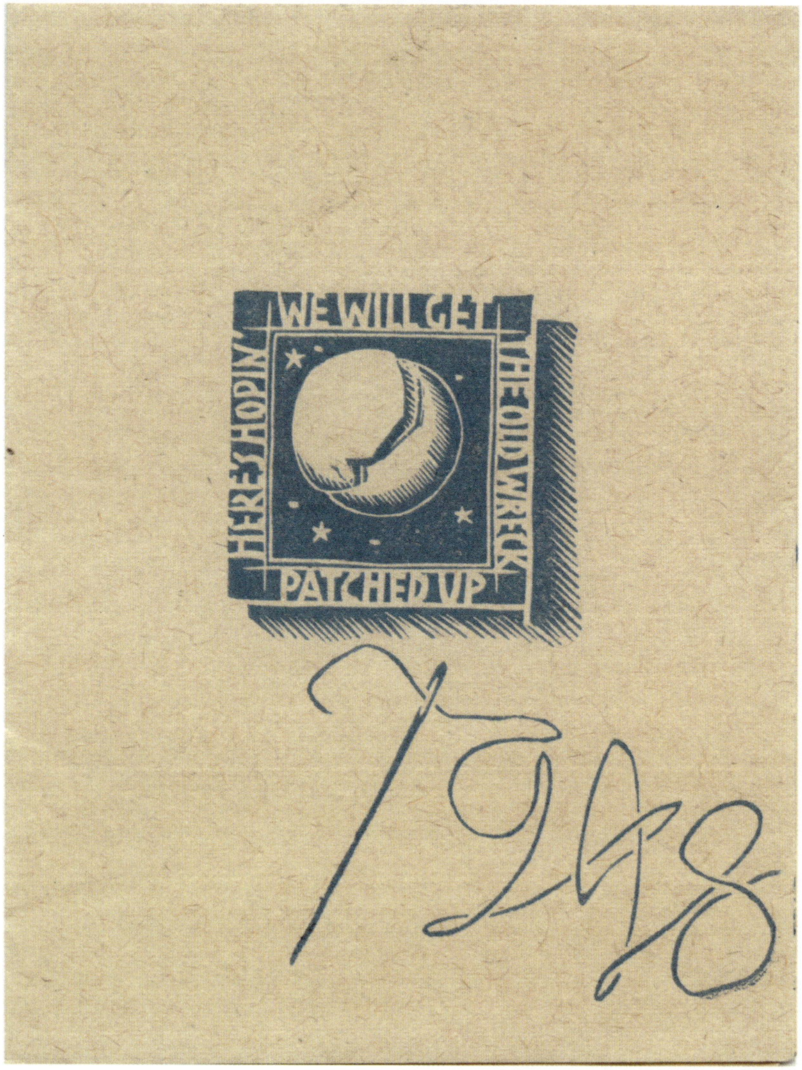

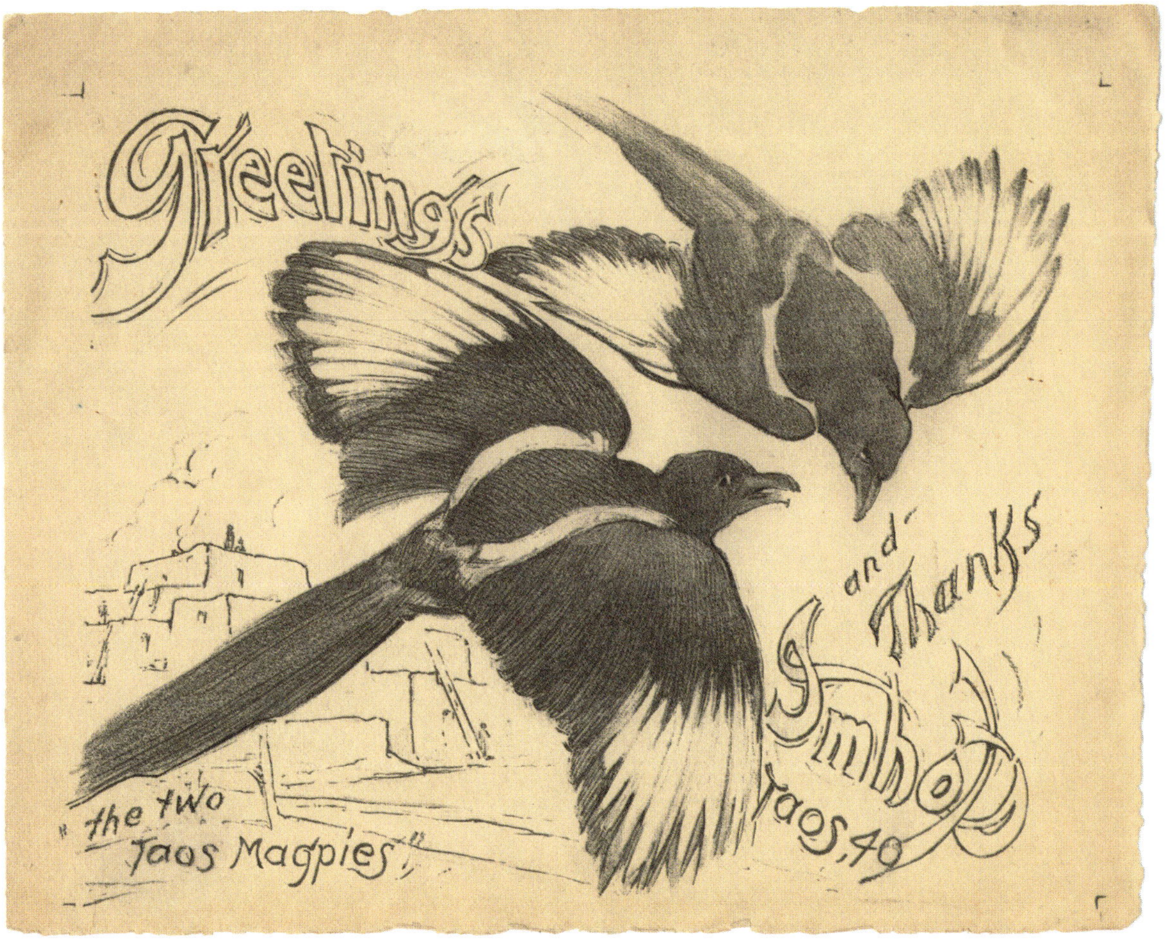

JOSEPH IMHOF. LITHOGRAPH. 1949

Imhof represents himself and his wife, Sally, as "the two Taos magpies." Magpies, which are omnipresent in Taos, are frequently seen in Native American myth as helpers or allies of humans.

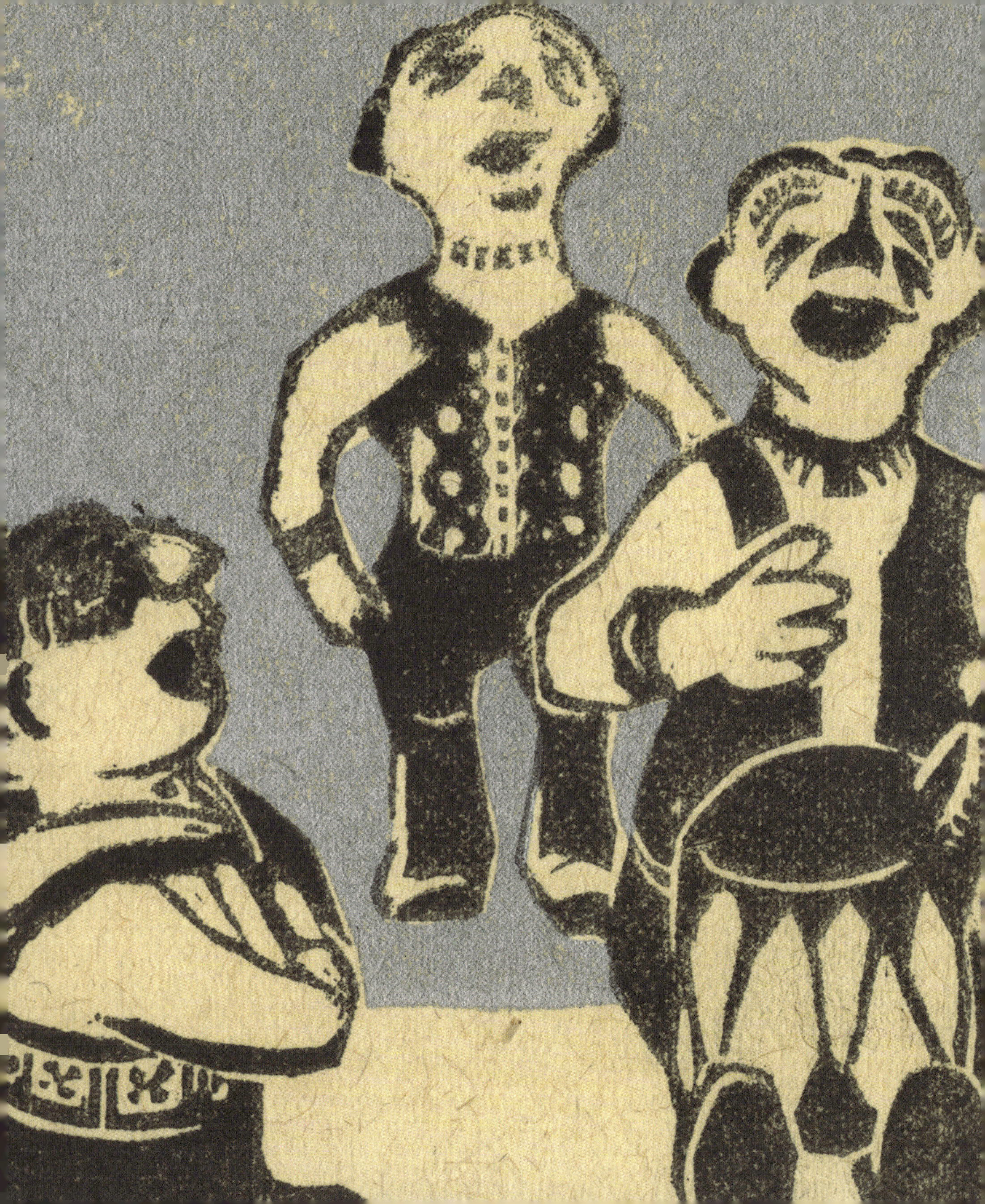

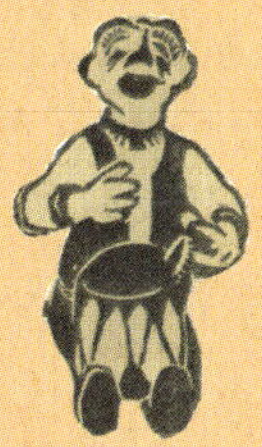

The 1950s years of prosperity were good for the artists in New Mexico. The New Mexico Fine Arts Museum thrived and frequently showed the work of local artists. The war in Korea was distant, the Civil Rights Movement was gaining momentum on the East Coast and in the South, and the Cold War was something one read about in the newspapers.

GUSTAVE BAUMANN. WOODCUT. 1950

Baumann writes doggerel verse in a New Year's greeting for a new decade with a foot-long card.

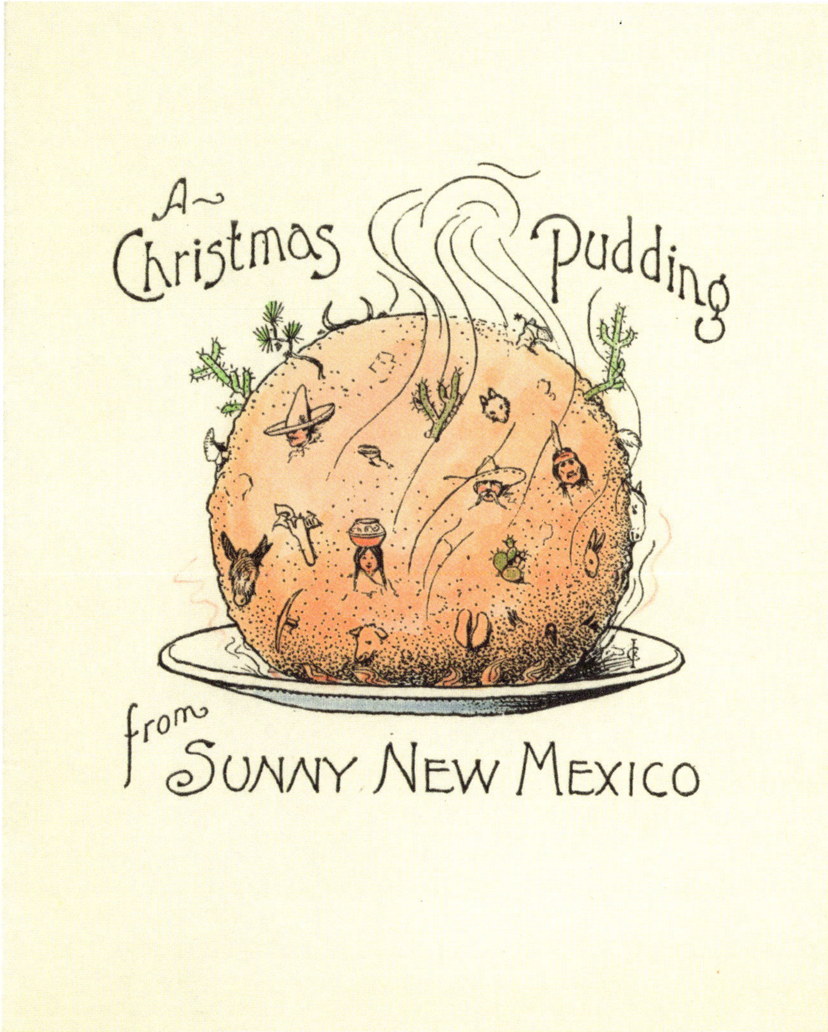

KENNETH CHAPMAN. WATERCOLOR DRAWING,
COMMERCIALLY PRINTED. 1953

An early arrival to the Santa Fe scene, artist and archaeologist Chapman reminisces by sending a reprint of his New Mexico Christmas Pudding, first sent fifty years before in 1903.

HELEN GREENE BLUMENSCHEIN.
SERIGRAPH. EARLY 1950S

Ernest Blumenschein writes a personal greeting to the Baumanns on a card created by his daughter.

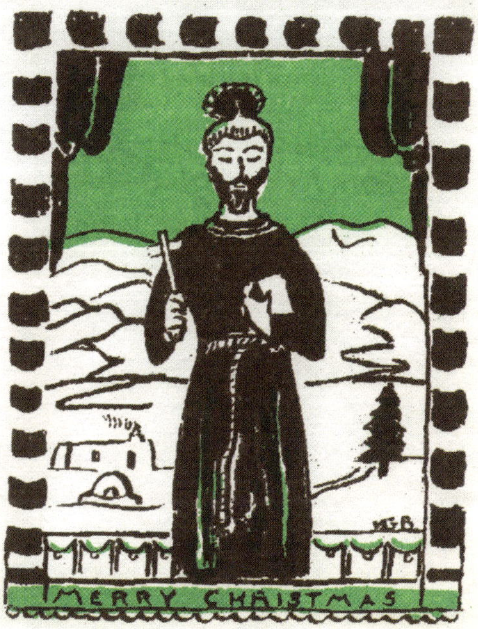

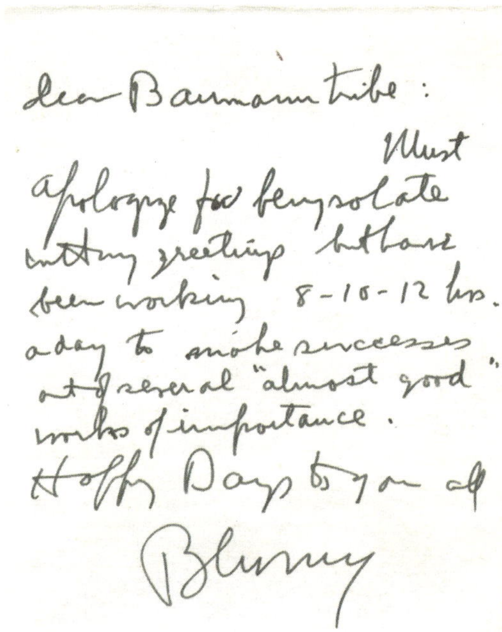

Dear Baumann tribe:

Must apologize for being so late with my greetings but have been working 8-10-12 hrs. a day to make successes out of several "almost good" works of importance.

Happy Days to you all

Blummy

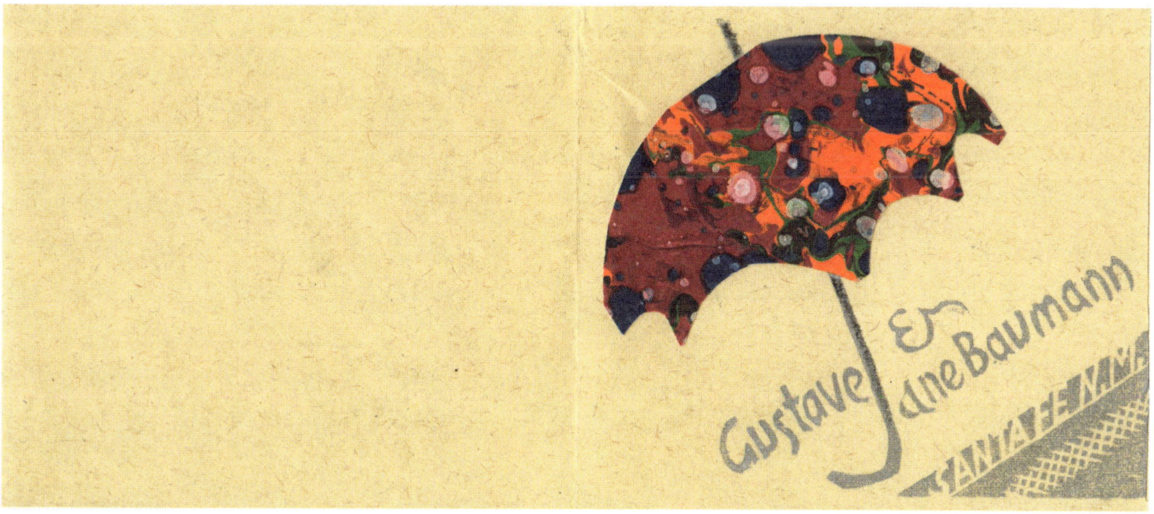

GUSTAVE BAUMANN. WOODCUT AND MARBLED PAPER COLLAGE. 1955

Santa Fe experienced historic drought in the 1950s. Gus is still hoping to use his umbrella.

THEODORE VAN SOELEN. COLOR WOODCUT. UNDATED, CA. 1950S

Van Soelen departs from his well-known paintings and lithographs of cowboy life in this formal depiction of an elegant carved door. The chile ristras and tiny evergreen trees flanking the door were painted by hand.

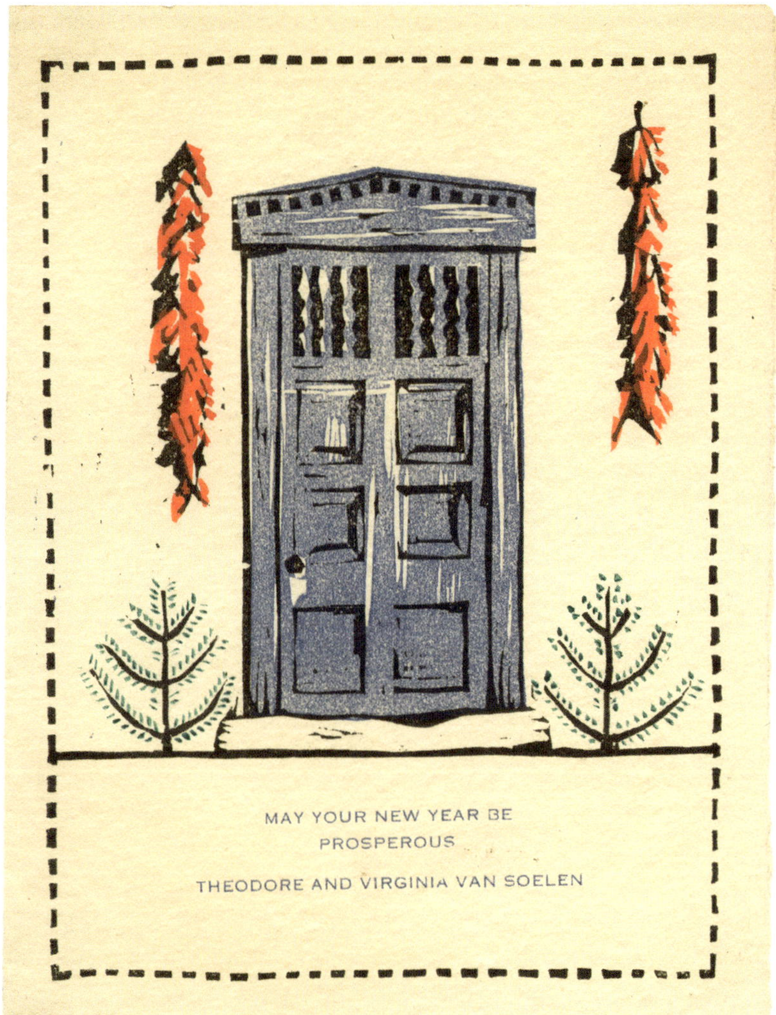

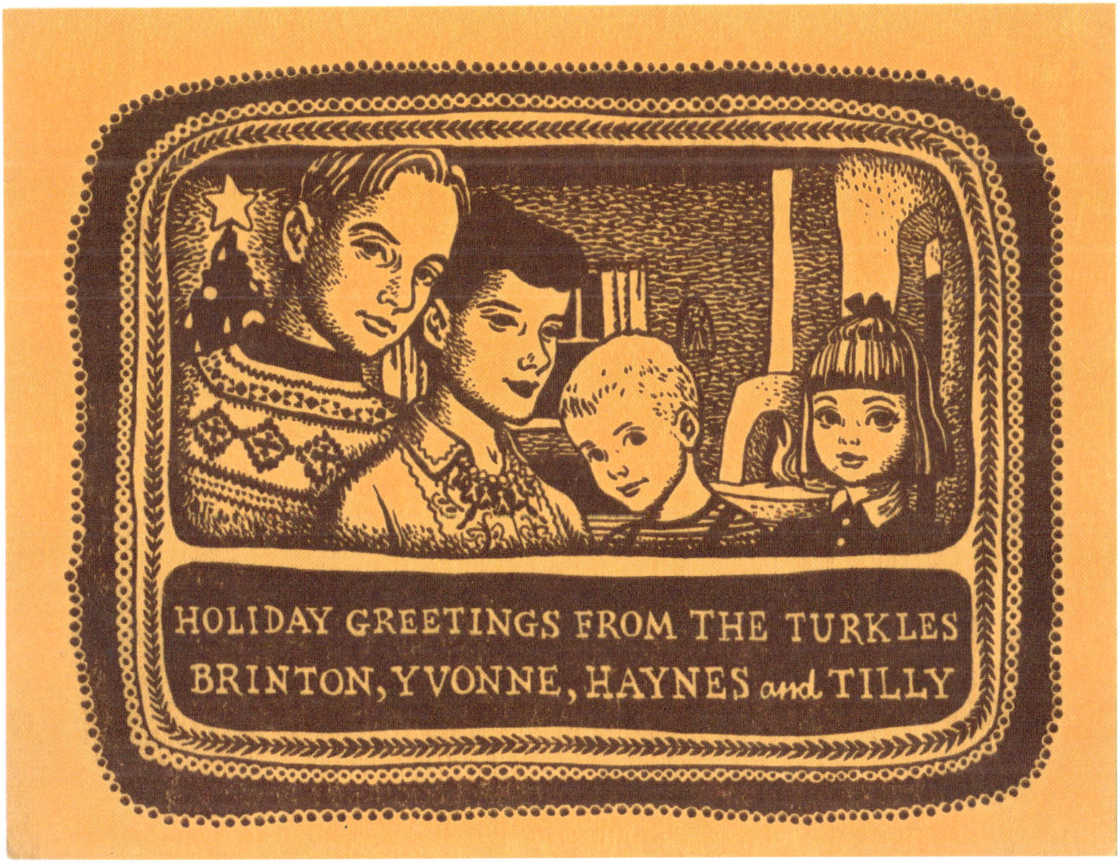

BRINTON TURKLE. WOODCUT. MID-1950S

Children's book illustrator Brinton Turkle poses his family in their typical New Mexico adobe house to create a portrait of holiday happiness.

GUSTAVE BAUMANN. COLOR WOODCUT. 1956

Baumann uses similar images, reconfigured and in different colors, to those in his 1946 color woodcut *Cochiti Ensemble.* The figures in the print are those of Cochiti pottery, but he makes his point with the pun on "Hopi" and "Happy."

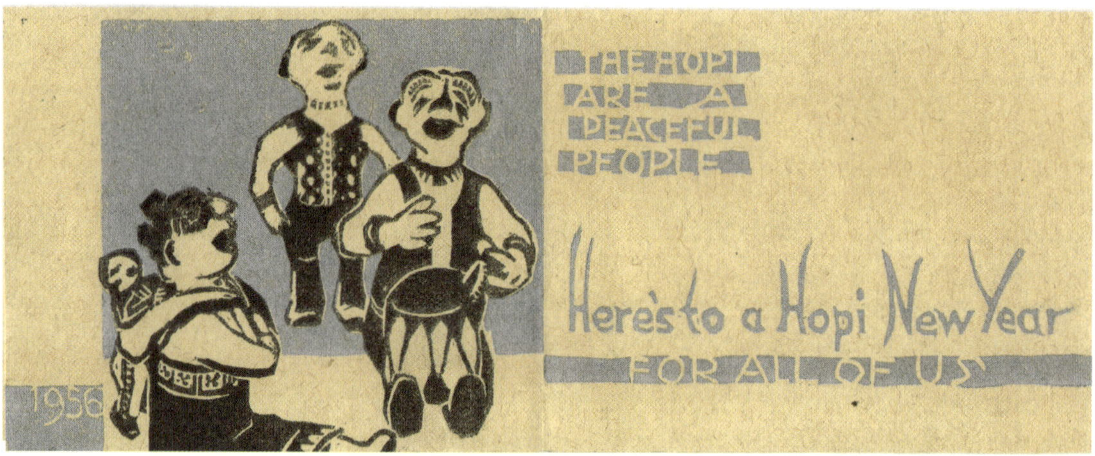

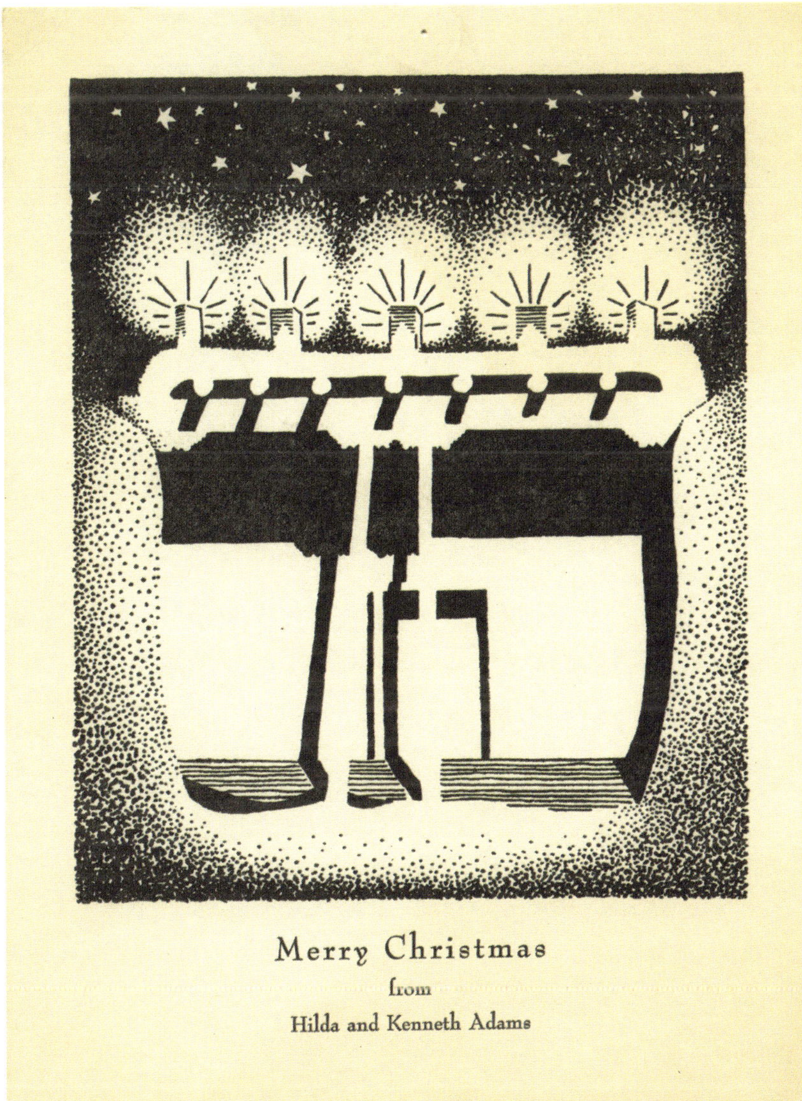

KENNETH ADAMS.
PHOTO-ENGRAVING
FROM INK DRAWING.
UNDATED, CA. 1950S

Taos painter and lithographer Kenneth Adams presents a starkly rendered view of the classic *portal* with *luminarias*.

CYRUS LEROY BALDRIDGE.
OFFSET LITHOGRAPHY
FROM INK DRAWING. 1950S

The amusing Santa Claus dancing on a snow-covered cactus is printed, but the personal salutation to Gus and Jane has been carefully entered by hand to appear as if it were part of the original printing.

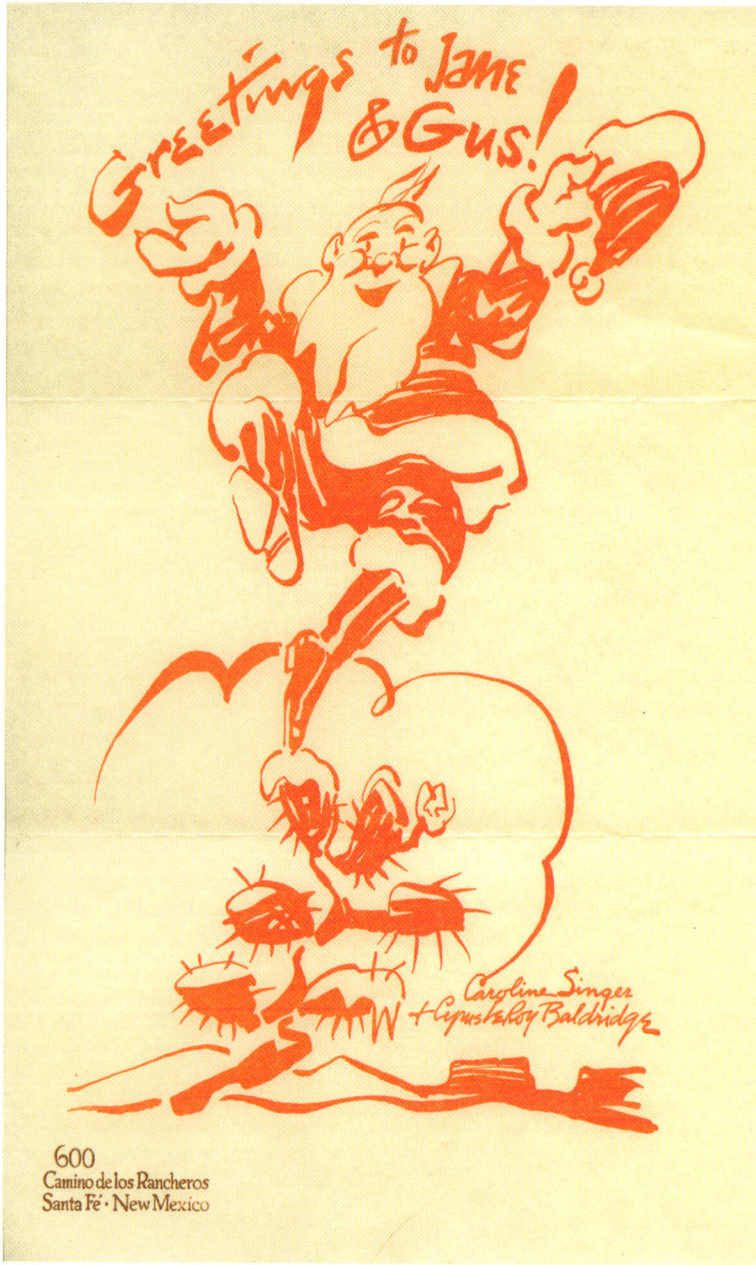

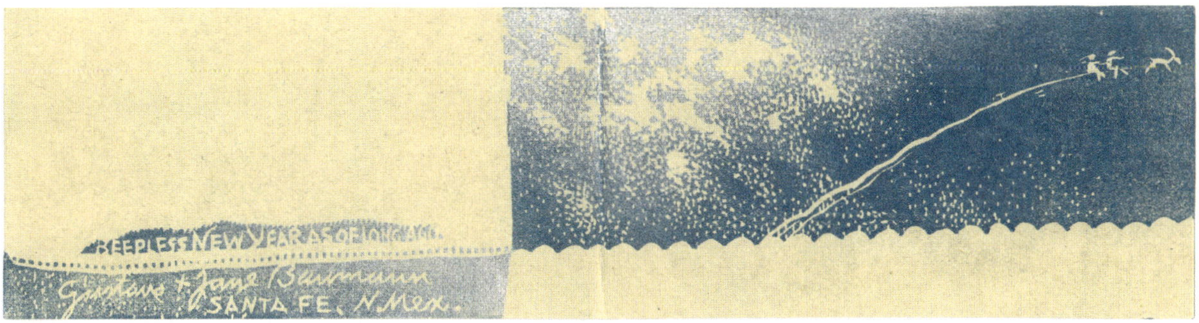

GUSTAVE BAUMANN. WOODCUT. 1957

Baumann picks up on the worldwide fascination with the Russian Sputnik. On October 4, 1957, the Soviet Union astonished the world with the launching of the first man-made satellite. Sputnik circled the globe every ninety-six minutes. Its beeping radio signals were rebroadcast by radio and TV stations around the world, exciting the imagination and feeding the anxieties of ordinary citizens everywhere.

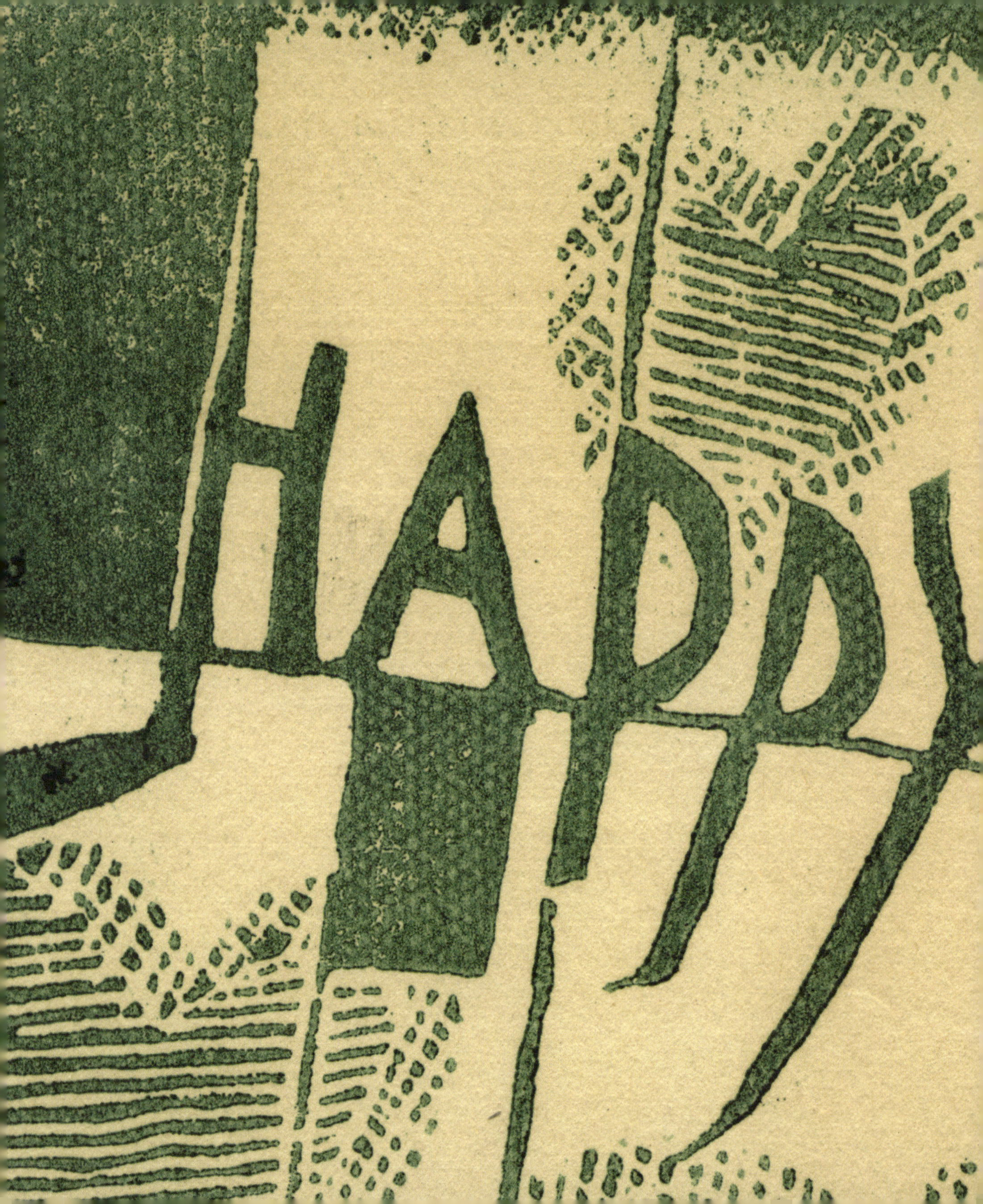
HAPP

By the 1960s and '70s the pace of change in the nation and the world seemed almost out of control. New Mexico saw an influx of hippies, and the war in Vietnam was beamed into living rooms. Man had truly gone to the moon. Santa Fe and Taos were hardly recognizable to the old-timers who remained. Indeed, few of the original artists of the "Golden Age" were still alive, and the group of friends exchanging cards with the Baumanns became ever smaller.

DOEL REED. PHOTO-ENGRAVING
FROM ORIGINAL DRAWING. 1961

Taos artist Doel Reed shows us not only the traditional adobe fireplace but a corner of his etching press.

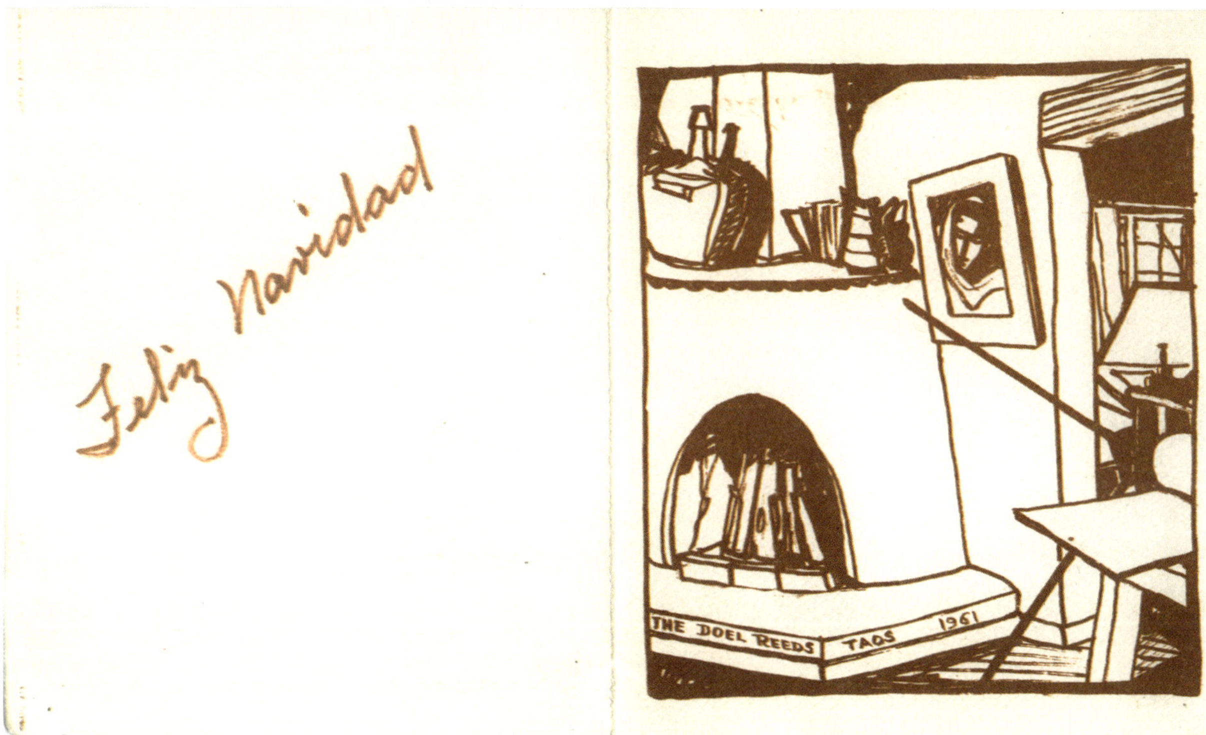

GUSTAVE BAUMANN.
WOODCUT. 1965

Baumann provides a token to cut out and keep in one's right shoe. This will apparently help to celebrate the holidays. Again, Baumann's humor can be a bit opaque.

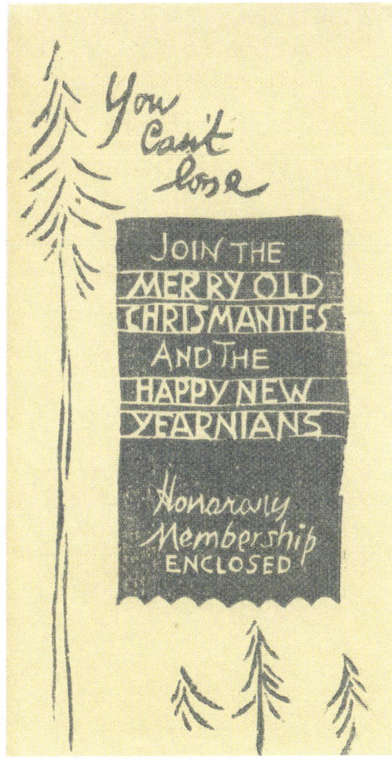

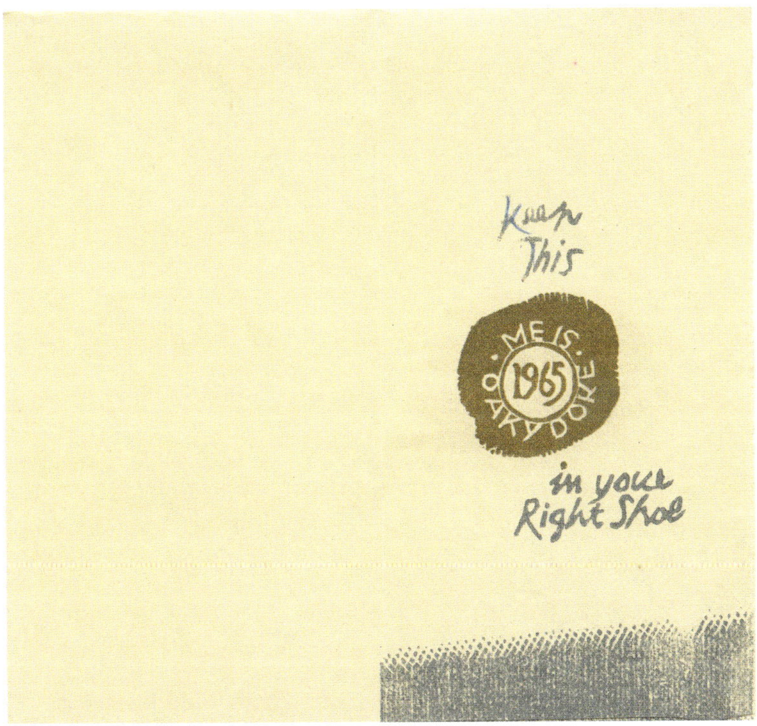

GUSTAVE BAUMANN.
WOODCUT. 1967

What made 1967 a "new era" and not just a new year?

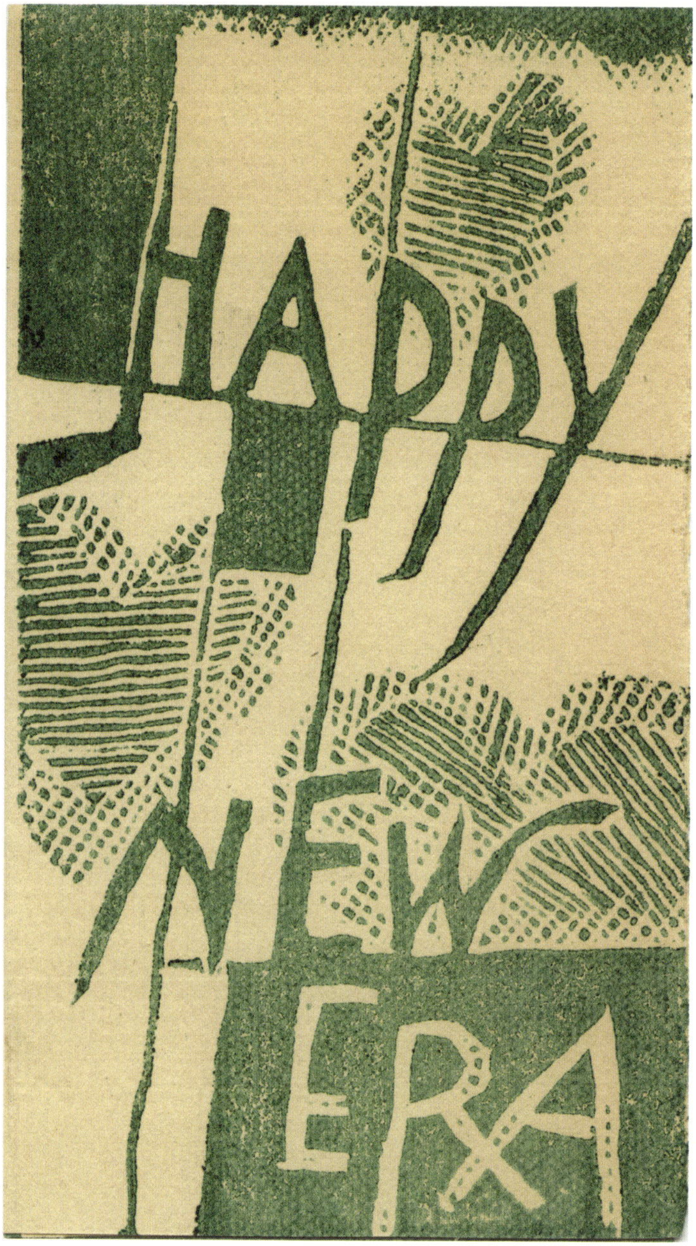

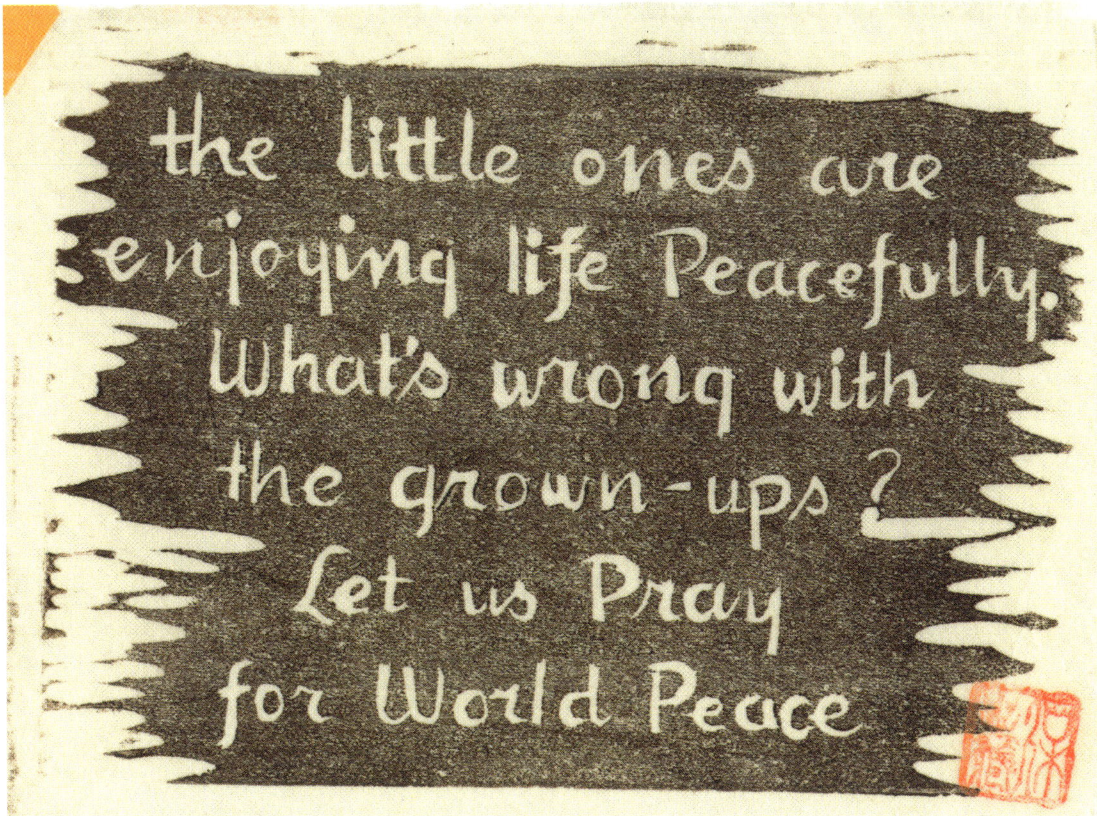

CHUZO TAMOTZU. WOODCUT. UNDATED

Probably created during the Vietnam War, this card reflects the extremely gentle nature of the Japanese-born painter, who lived in Santa Fe from 1948 until his death in 1975.

ALEXANDER BROOK.
PHOTO-ENGRAVING FROM
ORIGINAL PEN-AND-INK
DRAWING. UNDATED

Brook and his wife, former Santa Fe painter Gina Knee, send a charming, whimsically risqué Christmas card from their home in New York. Inside is a heartfelt letter from Gina to Jane Baumann recalling "wonderful memories of Santa Fe."

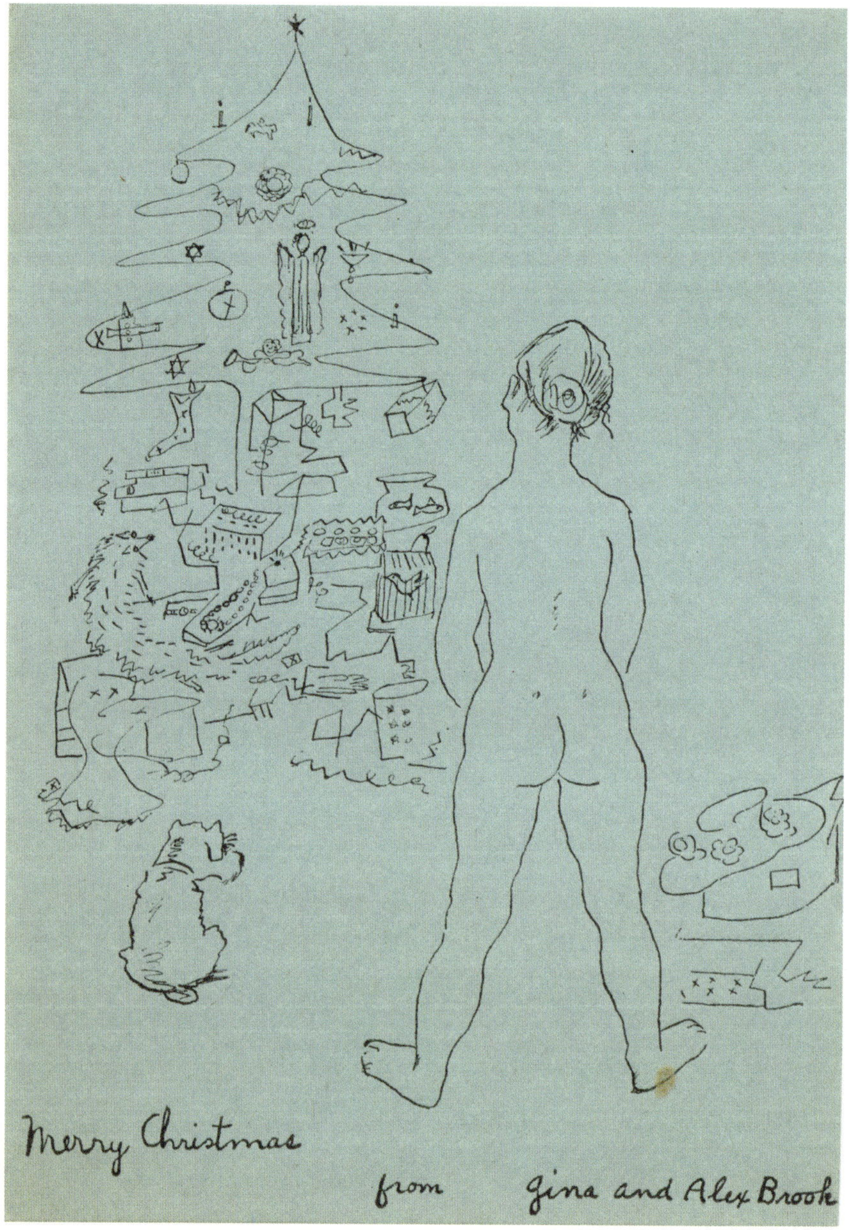

GUSTAVE BAUMANN. WOODCUT. 1970

This is Baumann's last holiday card. What might seem an ordinary phrase, "in one door and out the other," takes on prescience when one knows that Baumann died in the following year.

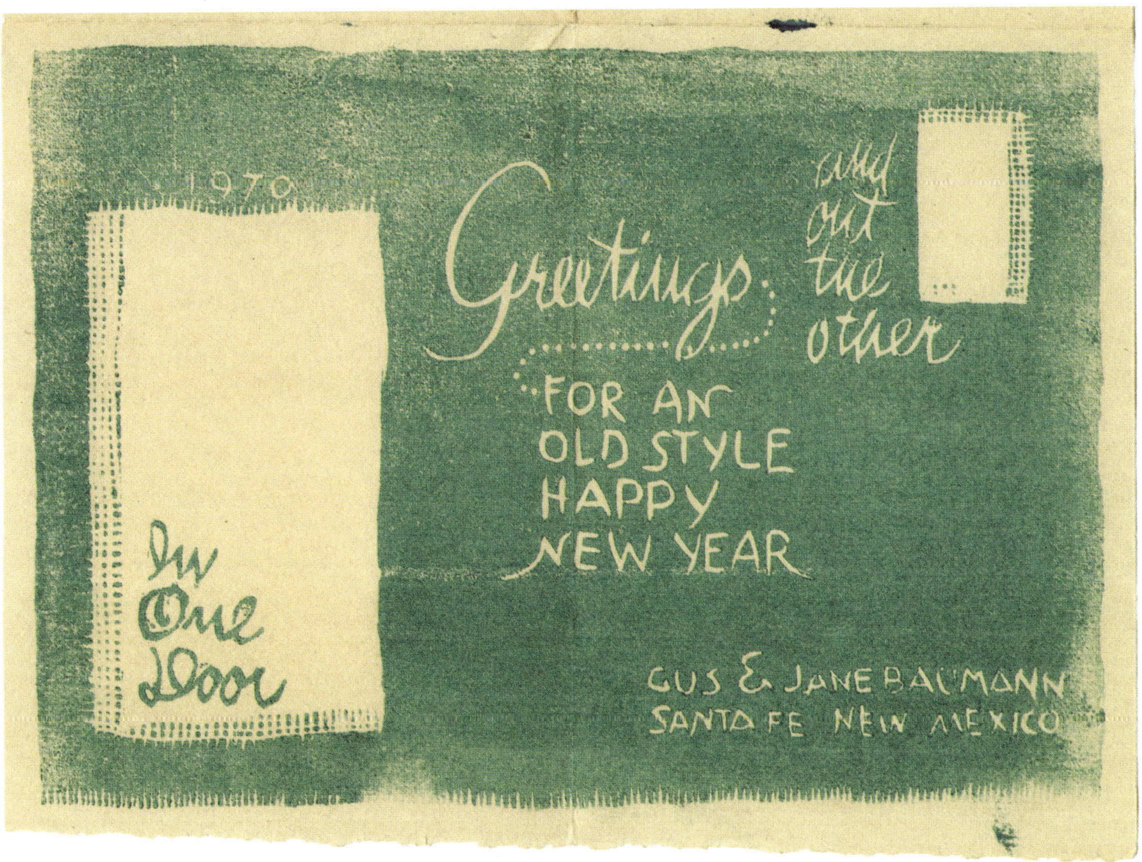

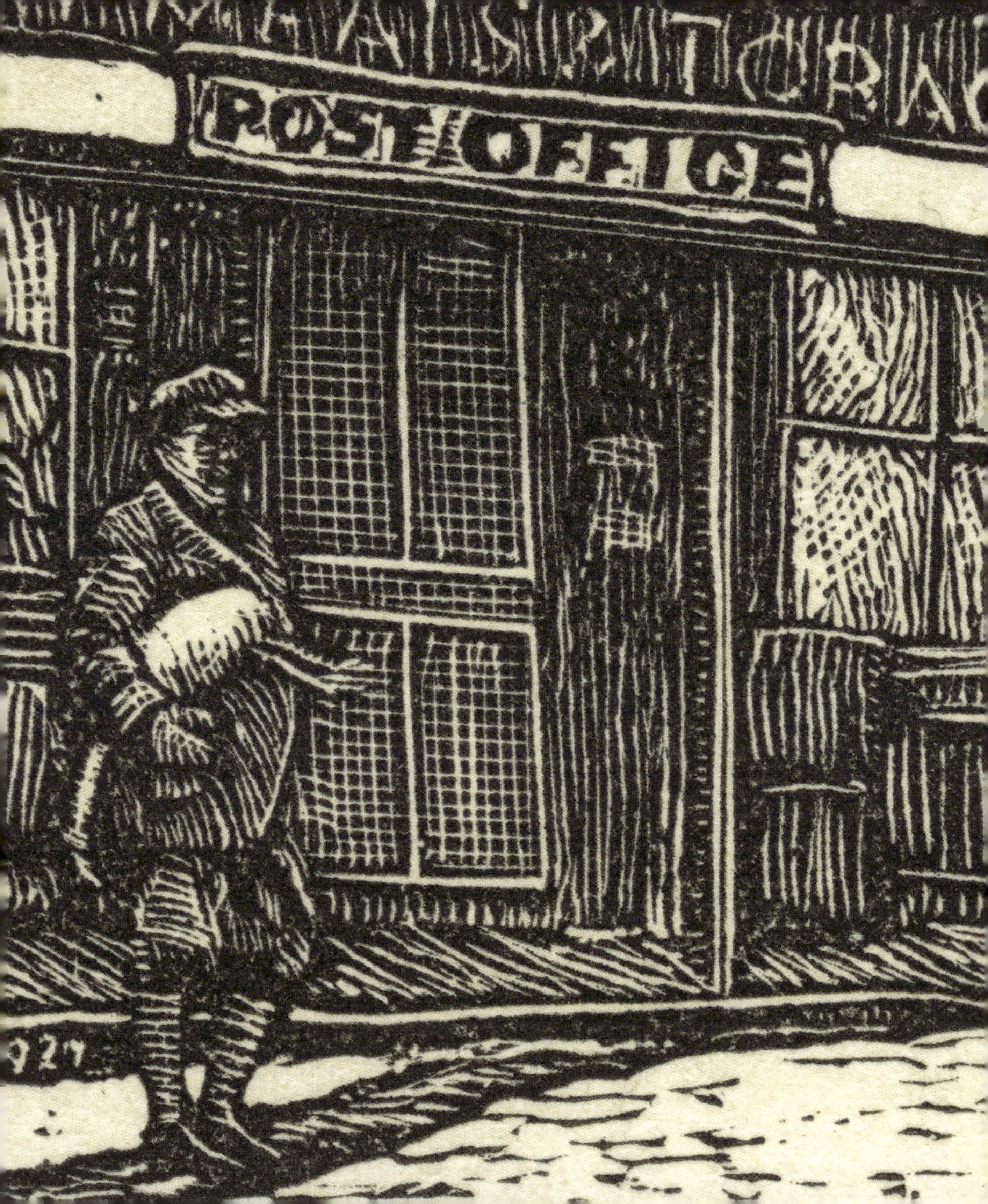
POST OFFICE

Year after year cards arrived for Gus and Jane Baumann from artist-friends beyond the colonies of Santa Fe and Taos. We close with a small selection from the hundreds of cards by artists whose reputations were made from far beyond New Mexico.

RUDOLPH RUZICKA. THREE-COLOR WOODCUT. 1916

Rudolph Ruzicka was another of the "Chicago apprentices" who went on to a distinguished career in the graphic arts. Baumann exchanged greetings throughout his life with his Czech-born friend. Ruzicka was a type design consultant for the Mergenthaler Linotype Company for fifty years. This card displays the delicate touch of the esteemed engraver, who in 1916 was also a proud new father.

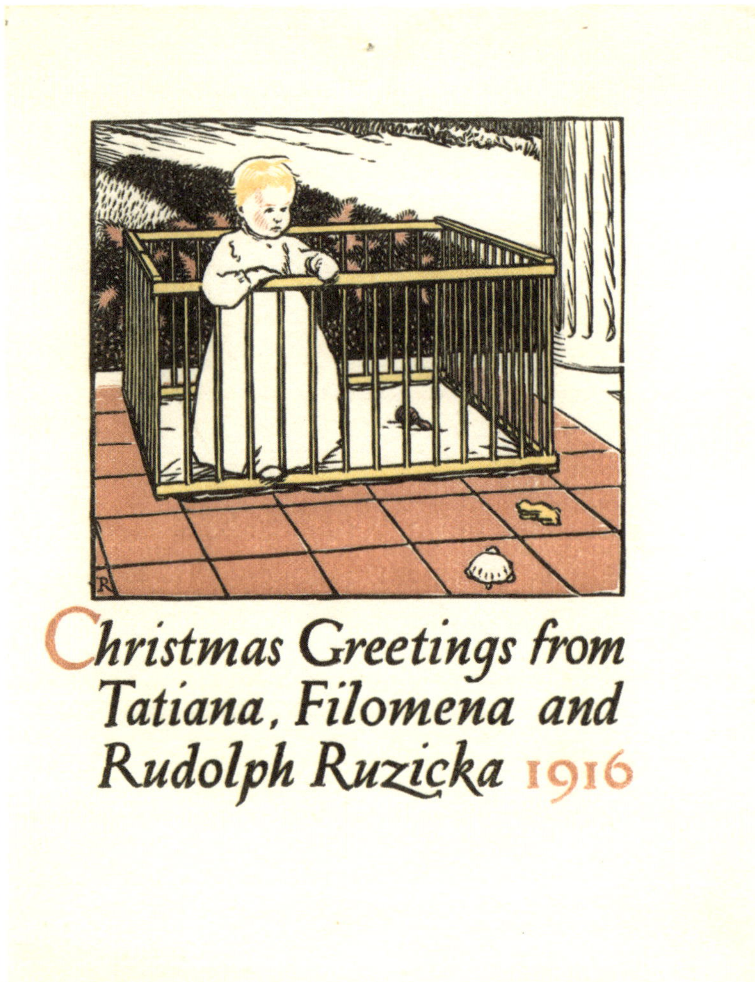

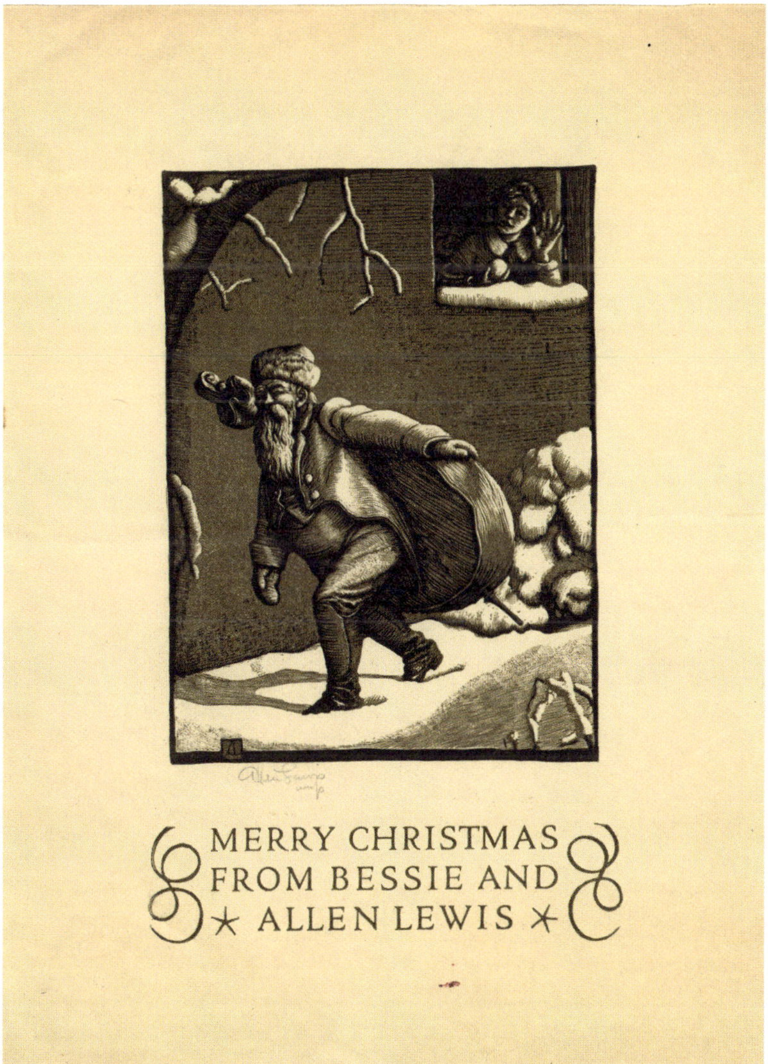

ALLEN LEWIS. TWO-COLOR WOODCUT. UNDATED

Allen Lewis and Gustave Baumann each won a gold medal at the 1915 Panama Pacific Exposition in San Francisco. Lewis was known for his artful book illustrations, color woodcuts and etchings, and as a photographer, becoming part of the Alfred Stieglitz circle.

J. J. LANKES, WOODCUT. 1927

Although close in age to Baumann, Lankes came to woodcut much later in his career. Lankes wrote to Baumann asking advice on how to get started in woodcut, and, in return, Baumann's advice paid off. Lankes, who documented rural Americana, became one of the most prolific and well-known woodcut artists of the 20th century.

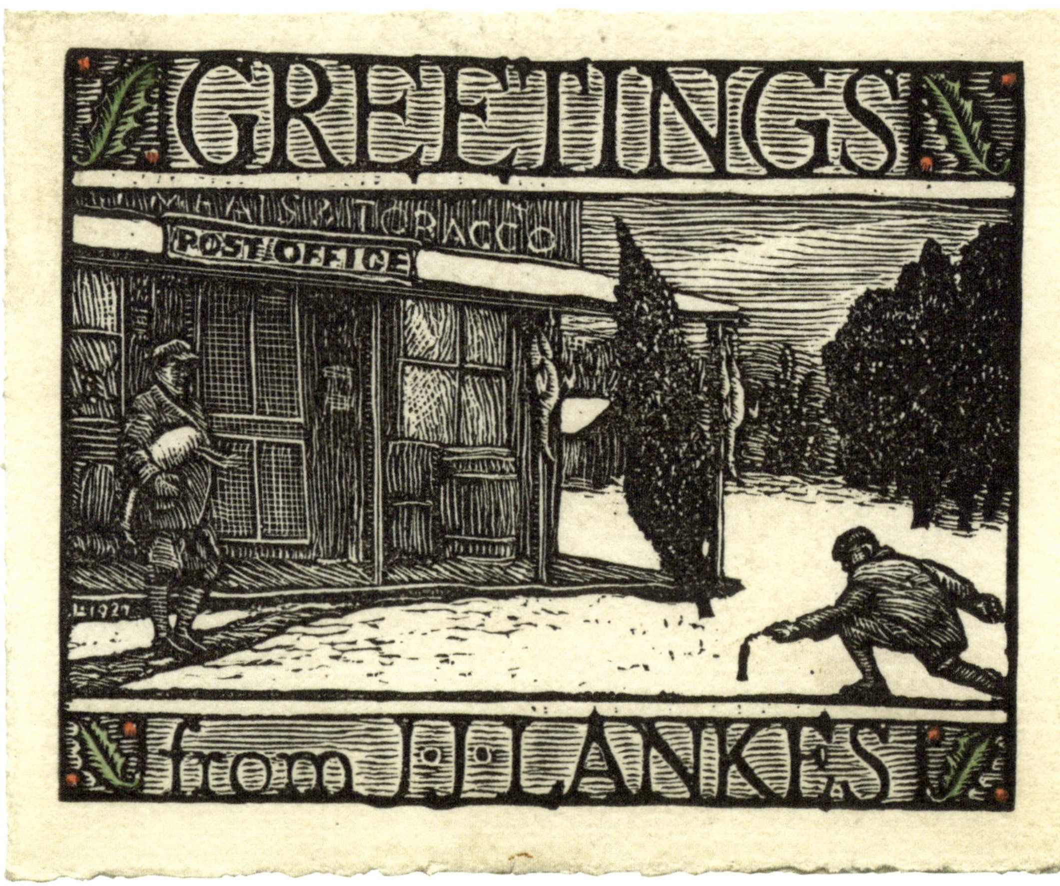

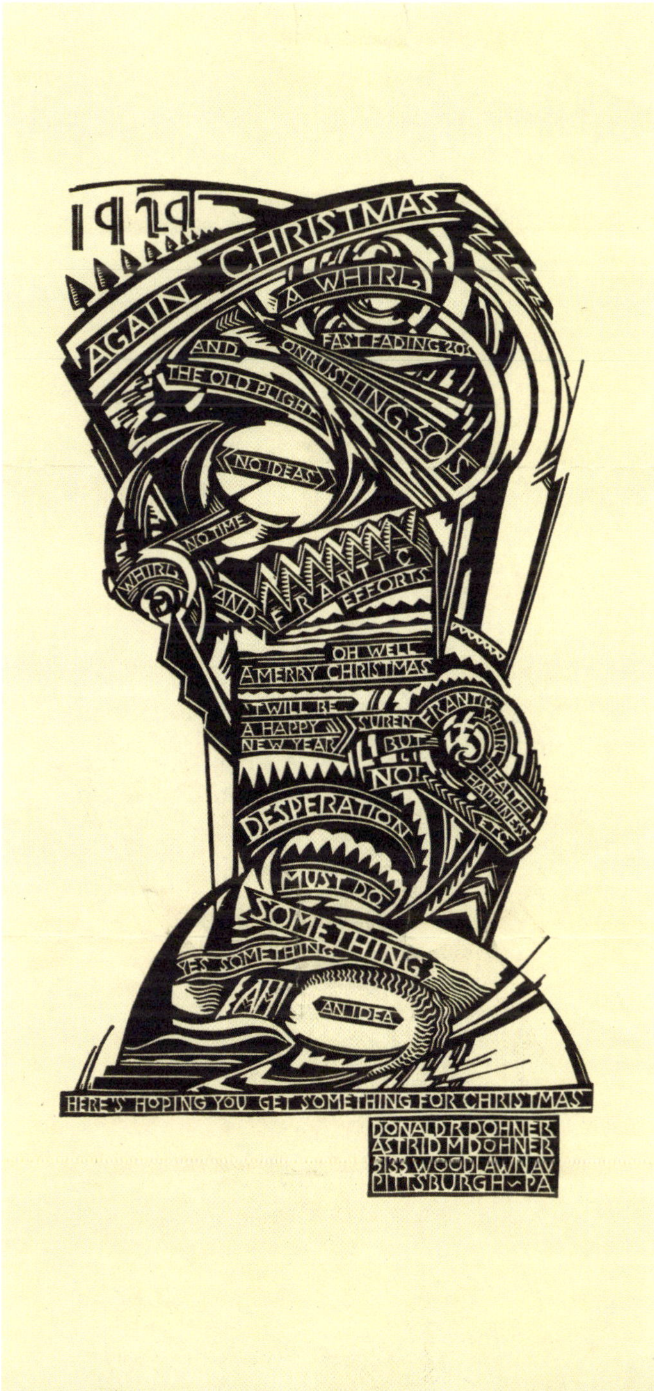

DONALD DOHNER. WOODCUT. 1929

This large card represents everything that the artists who came to New Mexico left behind: not only a frantic pace of life but, in this case, the stress that everyone felt following the Crash of '29. Coming from a similar Midwest art background as Baumann, Dohner's career traveled an opposite track. He pioneered the teaching of industrial design in America, designing everything from ashtrays to locomotives. In a sad twist of fate, Dohner died suddenly on Christmas 1943.

Suggested Reading

Hand of a Craftsman: The Woodcut Technique of Gustave Baumann, by David Acton. (Santa Fe: Museum of New Mexico Press, 1996.)

Will Shuster: A Santa Fe Legend, by Joseph Dispenza and Louise Turner. (Santa Fe: Museum of New Mexico Press, 1989.)

Willard Clark: Printer and Printmaker, by David Farmer. (Santa Fe: Museum of New Mexico Press, 2008.)

Gustave Baumann: Nearer to Art, by Martin F. Krause, Madeline Carol Yurtseven, and David Acton. (Santa Fe: Museum of New Mexico Press, 1993.)

Passions in Print: Private Press Artistry in New Mexico, 1834–Present, by Pamela S. Smith and Richard Polese. (Santa Fe: Museum of New Mexico Press, 1997.)

Gustave Baumann's Southwest, by Joseph Traugott. (Petaluma, CA: Pomegranate Communications, Inc., 2007.)

The Hand-Carved Marionettes of Gustave Baumann: Share Their World, by Ellen Zieselman; essay by Elizabeth Cunningham. (Santa Fe: Museum of New Mexico Press, 1999.)

Credits

Unless otherwise noted all illustrations are from the Fray Angélico Chávez History Library, New Mexico History Museum, Santa Fe.

Pg. 4 Gustave Baumann, Serigraph, 1946. New Mexico Museum of Art

Pg. 6 The Press at the Palace of the Governors (photographer unknown)

Pg. 18 Photograph by Blair Clark

Pg. 21 Courtesy of the Ann Baumann Trust

Pg. 23 School for Advanced Research, AC 18:412:45, photograph by W. Thomas McGrath

Pages 16, 26, 32, 35, 42, 44, 49, 67 New Mexico Museum of Art

Pg. 43 Fenyes-Curtin-Paloheimo Collection, Acequia Madre House

Pg. 53 Collection of Kevin Ryan

Pg. 68 The Academy for the Love of Learning

Pg. 77 Collection of Jerry West

Pages 80, 87 Bell Family Collection

Pg. 82 Collection of Nancy Wirth

Pg. 83 New Mexico Museum of Art Library and Archives

Graphic elements used in section openers are by Gustave Baumann.

 Museum of New Mexico Press is the publishing arm of the New Mexico Department of Cultural Affairs.

Project editor: Mary Wachs

Design and production: David Skolkin

Composition: Set in Brioso Pro

Manufactured in Canada

10 9 8 7 6 5 4 3 2

Library of Congress Cataloging-in-Publication Data

New Mexico History Museum.
Gustave Baumann and friends : artist cards from holidays past / by Jean Moss and Thomas Leech. -- First [edition].
pages cm
ISBN 978-0-89013-598-3 (clothbound : alk. paper) 1. Greeting cards—New Mexico--Santa Fe--Catalogs. 2. Artists—Correspondence—Catalogs. 3. Baumann, Gustave, 1881-1971—Correspondence—Catalogs. 4. Baumann, Gustave, 1881-1971—Friends and associates—Correspondence—Catalogs. 5. New Mexico History Museum—Catalogs. I. Moss, Jean, 1940- author. II. Leech, Thomas (Thomas Edward), author. III. Title.
NC1861.U6N496 2014
769.9789'56074--dc23
2014017717

Museum of New Mexico Press
Santa Fe, NM
mnmpress.org

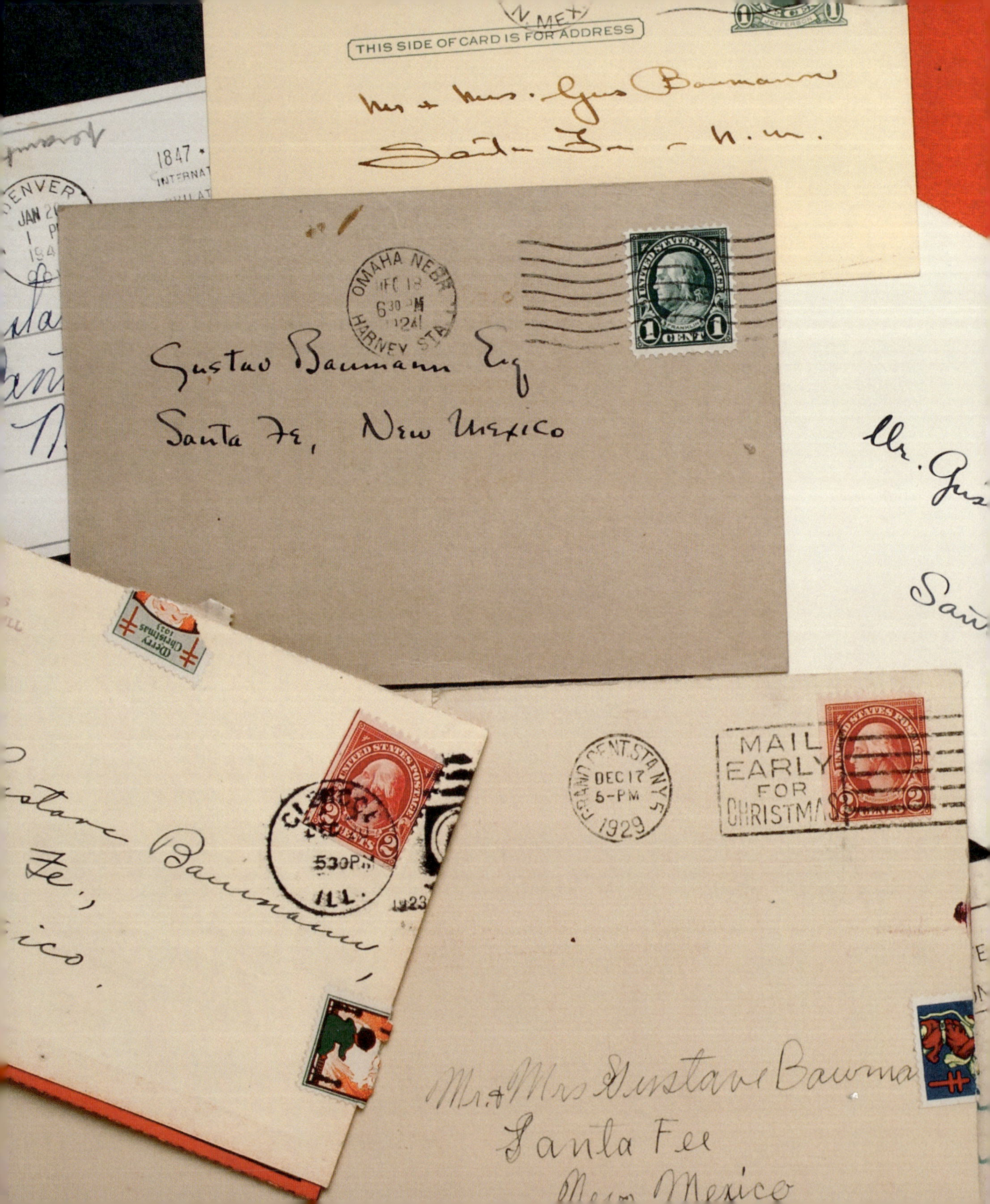
THIS SIDE OF CARD IS FOR ADDRESS
Mr + Mrs. Gus Baumann
OMAHA NEBR
DEC 18
6 30 PM
1924
HARNEY STA
Gustav Baumann Esq
Santa Fe, New Mexico
GRAND CENT. STA N.Y.
DEC 17
5-PM
1929
MAIL EARLY FOR CHRISTMAS
Mr + Mrs Gustave Bauma
Santa Fee
New Mexico